D1265290

# Power Praying

## Prayer That Produces Results

Jennifer Kennedy Dean

*6783*

*WinePress Publishing* **WP** *Mukilteo, WA 98275*

This book is dedicated to my mother, Audrey Kennedy—prayer mentor, prayer support, faith hero.

"Her children arise and call her blessed; her husband also, and he praises her: 'Many women do noble things, but you surpass them all'" (Prov. 31:28-29).

# Acknowledgment

Any book I write, any seminar I lead, anytime I speak—it's really a family project. Without my family's support and encouragement, I could not do what God has called me to do.

Thanks to my husband, Wayne, and our sons, Brantley, Kennedy, and Stinson.

You're the ones who put up with the inconveniences of having a "mom with a mission"— and you do it with grace and humor. I love you.

# Power Praying

"The prayer of a righteous man
is powerful and effective" (James 5:16).

# 1

# Do Your Prayers Have Power?

Do your prayers have power? When you pray, do you consistently see the power of God manifested on the earth? Does your experience in prayer match God's descriptions of prayer's power given in His Word?

"The prayer of a righteous man is powerful and effective," we read in James 5:16. Is that how you would define your prayer life— powerful and effective? The words "powerful and effective" are translated from a single Greek word meaning *capable of producing results; to have or exercise force*. Prayer, James says, has force and produces results. Prayer impacts lives and situations on the earth. True prayer works.

Many believers are discouraged about prayer. Secretly, many have reached the conclusion that prayer doesn't work or that prayer only works sometimes. Promises in the Bible regarding prayer seem unreliable, the outcome of prayer unpredictable. As a result, we have watered down or scaled back the scripture's descriptions of the power of prayer. We expect less from God than He longs to give. After all, how silly we felt having prayed boldly and with great conviction, believing with all our might, only to see our prayers go unanswered. Our faith takes a hit from which it never recovers. Next time, we are more circumspect with our requests. Next time, our expectations are more in line with reality.

Having reached this point, we need to look for ways to explain away the power promised in scripture. Attempting to justify the lack of powerful praying, we have tried to reduce prayer to an activity that will match our experience, rather than looking for the source of prayer's failure in ourselves.

Suppose you consult a doctor about an ailment and he prescribes a medication. Imagine that the doctor promises that this medication will cure your ailment. "Take this medicine in the prescribed dosage three times a day every day for ten days," he instructs. Suppose that you go home and follow his instructions for a few days. You see little or no improvement, so you begin to doubt the efficacy of the medicine. You take it haphazardly and finally quit taking it at all. When you return to the doctor for a check-up, you say, "That medicine didn't cure me as you promised it would." Is your accusation accurate? Did the medicine fail? Of course the medicine did not cure your illness. You didn't apply it correctly. You made your own rules. You wanted the medicine to work on your terms. The failing is not in the medicine but in your method of applying the medicine.

This is a picture of how we have come to think of prayer. "Prayer doesn't work like the Bible says it will work," we say. Why not? Could it be because we have tried to make prayer work on our terms and that the failure is not with prayer itself but with our way of praying? Remember that God's Word clearly states that God's power produces results on the earth when a righteous person prays. (James 5:16)

As you read this book, I challenge you to look at your prayer life honestly and without pretense. I ask you to set aside your past experiences that have caused you to feel disillusioned about prayer and its effects. Would you be open to God's Word as He speaks it through His Spirit into your understanding? In response to His Word, are you willing to change the way you view prayer? Would you put your life at His disposal and give Him access to your mind so that He can bring understanding?

## Practice Power Praying

"The unfolding of your words gives light; it gives understanding to the simple" (Ps. 119:130).

The "unfolding" of God's Word brings light, or understanding. Imagine that you were given a piece of paper upon which was written information you needed. Imagine that the person handing you that paper had folded it as tightly as it could be folded so that it was reduced in size to one square inch. How would you discover the important information on that paper? You would unfold it. As you unfold it, more and more of the information becomes readable. If you tried to discern the information without unfolding the paper, you would never discover the knowledge available inside.

So it is with God's Word. God will unfold His Word. Listening to Him, you will discover that what may look like one little sentence, phrase, or word, when He unfolds it, is a wealth of wisdom and knowledge. Don't just read the surface. Wait for the unfolding.

**Make this prayer your own:**

Today's date _____

*Father:*

*I want You to unfold Your Word to me. I want to know what lies under the surface. I want understanding. So I come to you simply—with my mind open and eager to follow Your Spirit into all Truth, leaving behind all error and misunderstanding.*

*In Jesus' Name.*

Don't be afraid to be honest with God. Listen to what Job said when he felt disillusioned with God: "I will give free reign to my complaint and speak out in the bitterness of my soul" (Job 10:1). God did not condemn Job for his openness, but instead complimented him for speaking right. (Job 42:7-8) It was Job's honesty with himself before God that opened the way for God to reach him with the truth.

As you begin this journey to understand how to pray with power, what past experiences with prayer are holding you back? Stop now and name them. Commit all these experiences, struggles, and longings to the Father. Don't let them hold you back any longer. Instead, let them propel you forward. Invite God to use these experiences as entry points where He can bring light. Trust Him. He is the one and only prayer teacher, and it is His joy and delight to teach you to pray.

## Misconceptions About Prayer

Misconceptions about prayer limit us. These misunderstandings are perhaps not articulated, but they are obvious in our approach to prayer and our expectations about prayer. The truth about prayer will free us to pray with the boldness God intends.

**(1) Some pray as if prayer is the way to get "things" from God.**

Does God tell us to ask Him for the material things we need? Yes, He does. Is it wrong to ask God for material things? No, God encourages it. However, this is not the primary purpose for which God ordained prayer. If your prayer life is limited to placing your orders with God and expecting Him to fulfill them in a timely manner, I imagine you have often been disappointed.

Prayer for material needs is presented by Jesus as the very simplest kind of prayer. This kind of prayer requires the least amount of spiritual energy. Jesus teaches, first of all, that your Father knows what you need before you ask Him.[1] Then He goes on to tell His followers that they do not have to worry about what to eat or what to wear. He points us to nature and the splendor with which the Father clothes the lilies of the field and the care with which He watches the birds of the air. He says, speaking of material things, "Your Father knows that you need them." You do not have to convince Him of your need. Not only does He know your need, He also cares about your need. You are more important to Him than the birds and the lilies. His provision for them is ample evidence that He will provide for you. You do not have to persevere and struggle in prayer for material needs. Since that's the case, you can focus on seeking His kingdom and His righteousness, certain that your needs will be met.[2]

> Jesus said, "I tell you the truth, unless you change and become like little children, you will never enter the kingdom of heaven" (Matt. 18:3). To see the kingdom of God clearly, one must leave behind adult pretenses and sophisticated arguments. Often, we come to God prepared to do battle with Him, convince Him of the validity of our need and give Him reasons to meet it.
>
> What a contrast to the way a little child comes to his or her parents. A child simply assumes

that the need or desire is potent enough to speak for itself. All that is required is to bring that need to Mom or Dad's attention. The request assumes the answer. The child's only thought is to bring the need to the source of supply.

You don't need to build a theological case for why God should want to meet your need. He wants to meet your need because He's your Daddy and you are the apple of His eye. Jesus highlights the simplicity of supplication by saying, "Ask and it will be given to you...For everyone who asks receives" (Matt. 7:7-8). The Greek word translated "ask" is used to ask for something to be given, not done. It is the simplest, most straight-forward picture of asking for something you need.
(*Heart's Cry*, Jennifer Kennedy Dean)[3]

When a person seeks to use prayer merely as a means of obtaining material things, either needs or desire, that person will never discover the overwhelming and awe-inspiring power available through prayer. It is very simple for God to supply your material needs and He does so willingly.

**(2) Some pray as if prayer will give God new information or inspire in Him new ideas.**

Some approach prayer as if it is the responsibility of the petitioner to decide what God needs to do and then talk Him into doing it. This kind of pray-er sees himself as constantly having to overcome God's objections, or His inertia, or His procrastination. This person feels that God always starts out against him and must be won over. Prayer of this kind pits the prayer against God. It feels like a battle of wills.

As with every misconception about prayer, this error causes the praying person to expend spiritual energy, needlessly. The person who prays in this way tends to look for the right formula, or the right words to say, or the right order in which to say them. This person is always on a quest to find the approach to God that will finally get Him to act.

This person believes the myth that it is hard to get God to answer prayer. The truth is that God longs to do His work on earth in response to prayer. Prayer is His idea. God thought up prayer, not man.

God answers prayer, but He doesn't follow instructions. God reprimands, even ridicules, those who attempt to instruct Him. "Who has understood the mind of the Lord, or instructed him as his counselor? Whom did the Lord consult to enlighten him, and who taught him the right way? Who was it that taught him knowledge or showed him the path of understanding?" (Is. 40:13-14). However, He loves our prayers. He rejoices in them. They bring Him pleasure. They are a sweet-smelling aroma to Him.[4]

Power praying happens when God who longs to give is met by man who longs to receive His gift. God is the initiator. He made the promises and invited the petition. The secret to power praying lies not in how to ask, but in how to receive.[5]

> **(3) Some pray as if God sometimes forgets or tries to renege on His promises and is depending on pray-ers to remind Him of them.**

God does not need to be reminded of His promises. He made promises and bound Himself to us in a blood-sealed covenant so that we would know exactly what we could expect from Him. The purpose of His promises is to give us confidence and peace. Instead, sometimes we pray as if we are responsible for finding the scriptural promise that can be construed as guaranteeing the outcome we have prescribed, then taking that promise to God to hold Him to His Word.

This kind of pray-er treats God's Word as if it were a catalog. He decides what God should do, looks through the Bible to find a verse that will match his plan, and orders it. In doing so, as in catalog shopping, the pray-er skims over everything that holds no appeal. He picks and chooses.

Remember, scripture is not Gods *words*; it is God's *Word*. Scripture is a whole and cannot be cut apart and pasted together to match my agenda. His Word is not a catalog. It is His promise in writing.

When we approach prayer this way—as if God might try to get out of meeting our need, but since we have His promise, we can hold Him to it—we become drained of energy and suffer from prayer-fatigue. What a burden it is for me to search the scripture and find exactly the right verse to bring to God's attention. Instead, as I turn my heart and my mind toward Him, He reminds me of His promises. He reminds me of what I can count on. The promises are not for me to use in getting my way with God, but they are for God to use to inspire faith and confidence within me.

**(4) Some pray as if prayer is the means of cajoling God into releasing His carefully hoarded riches.**

Someone has said, "Prayer is not overcoming God's reluctance, but laying hold of God's willingness." God offers us His resources. He invites us to take His gifts. He does not have to be convinced to let go of His blessings. His Word says that He lavishes on us the riches of His grace (Eph. 1:8) and that He lavishes His love on us (1 John 3:1). He is extravagant in His gifts. He pours them out. Scripture never uses language that would portray God as stingy or hesitant to give. Instead we read that He "richly blesses all who call on him" (Rom. 10:12).

When we pray this way, we expend spiritual energy needlessly trying to convince God of something He's already convinced of. Giving you every good thing gives Him joy; it delights Him. Jesus assures us with these words: "'Do not be afraid, little flock, for your Father has been pleased to give you the kingdom'" (Luke 12:32). His heart is set on you to do you good.

## The Truth About Prayer

The truth about prayer will set you free. Prayer is the means by which you will be freed from your earth-bound, time-bound thinking to participate in eternity. True prayer releases His power so that His power can accomplish immeasurably more than we can ask or even imagine (Eph. 3:20).

God's power, the power released by prayer, is power that has a direct and observable impact on the earth. Paul describes it in Ephesians 1:19-21: "...His incomparibly great power for us who believe. That power is like the working of His mighty strength which He exerted in Christ when He raised him from the dead and seated Him at His right hand in the heavenlies."

God's power, which is beyond comparison, is available for "us who believe." The same power that raised Jesus from the dead; the same power that lifted Jesus above all rule and authority; that same power—"the working of His mighty strength"—is released in the material realm through prayer.

God means for prayer to always bring His power to earth. His intent is that every prayer find His "yes." "For the Son of God, Jesus Christ, ...was not 'Yes' and 'No'; but in him it has always been 'Yes.' For no matter how many promises God has made, they are 'Yes' in Christ" (1 Cor. 1:19-20).

Prayer will work as God intends for it to work when it becomes what God intends for it to be. Prayer is not an activity, but a relationship. Prayer is not a formula, but a life. Only when we have learned how to live prayer, breathe prayer, be prayer—only then will the power available through prayer be consistently manifested on the earth. God has ordained that prayer will be the conduit through which His intervening, earth-changing power flows from heaven to earth. Prayer is what sets God's will in motion on the earth.

When Jesus' disciples asked Him, "Lord, teach us to pray," Jesus gave them a prayer outline that we call The Lord's Prayer. In that outline Jesus included this petition: "Your kingdom come, your will be done, on earth as it is in heaven" (Matt. 6:10). Remember, Jesus didn't waste words. Every word He spoke came from the Father. These words, then, are important. The prayer teacher Himself spoke them. Would He have included this portion in the outline if God's kingdom would come and God's will would be done without my praying it? This portion of Jesus' teaching on prayer shows me conclusively that I must pray God's will done.

What did Jesus mean by "your kingdom come"? Was He talking about the final setting up of the kingdom? Jesus spoke of the kingdom primarily in terms of the present. He often said that now that He had come to earth, the kingdom of God had come to earth. He taught that the kingdom exists present-tense in believers. The kingdom of God is present where the rule of God is operative.[6] We might translate His statement, "Let Your sovereign rule take direct effect in this particular circumstance. Bring Your perfect will in this circumstance to earth by Your power in Your way. Do Your will on earth the same way You've already done it in heaven."[7] Prayer brings the power of God to earth to do the will of God.

Let's examine this thought more closely. You may be asking,"Is God's power ever absent from the earth?" The answer is "no." His power is never absent. He fills heaven and earth. The earth and its fullness belong to Him. The heavens declare His glory, and creation pours forth knowledge of Him. God's power covers the earth.[8]

God's specific and intervening power is released into circumstances and lives by prayer. Think of it like this. The sun's rays cover the earth. However, when one holds a magnifying glass over a flammable object, such as a dry leaf, the sun's rays are refracted (bent toward one another) through the glass. The result is that the rays of the sun are concentrated and directed, their power magnified. The refracted rays create focused and intense heat. The leaf, exposed to the focused power of the sun, bursts into flames.

The sun's rays are focused and directed, their power
magnified, through a convex lens such as a
magnifying glass.

God's power covers the earth. Prayer focuses and
magnifies His power on a particular life or situation.
"The Lord be magnified, Who delights in the prosperity
of His servant." (Psalm 35:27, NASB)

God's power covers the earth. Prayer focuses and magnifies His power on a particular situation or a specific life. That life or situation, consistently exposed to His intense power, is changed by it.

When the sun's rays are captured and refracted through the magnifying glass, has the glass increased or in any way changed the sun's power? No, it has only focused it. The power belongs only to the sun. So it is that prayer focuses the power of God.

## Practice Power Praying

"'Power and might are in your hand, and no one can withstand you'" (2 Chron. 20:6).

Where is God's power? It's in His hand. It's at the ready. It's immediately available. God's hand is the picture of His intervening, specific help. "Praise be to the Lord, the God of Israel, who with his hands has fulfilled what he promised with his mouth" (2 Chron. 6:4).

Is God's power limited in any way? No, it's limitless. No one can withstand Him. When exposed to the focused and intense power of God, no one can withstand that power. No one will be unaffected. No one will stay the same.

**Make this prayer your own:**

Today's date _____

*Father,*

*When I consider Your power, the ultimate power, the only power... and when I see Your power focused on my concern... I can only watch expectantly for how You will do Your work in Your way in Your time. What do I have to fear? In Jesus' Name.*

"This power is so rich and so mobile that all we have to do when we pray is to point to the persons or things to which we desire to have this power applied, and He, the Lord of this power, will direct the necessary power to the desired place at once." (*Prayer*, O. Hallesby)[9]

Power praying is simple, not complicated. It is as simple as pointing to where we are asking God to apply His power. God is holding out the promises. God is offering His power. God is the initiator, we are the responders. Power praying is receiving what God is offering.

[1]Matthew 6:8

[2]Matthew 6:25-34

[3]Jennifer Kennedy Dean, *Heart's Cry: Principles of Prayer* (New Hope, Birmingham, AL, 1992), pp. 67-68.

[4]Revelation 5:8; Psalm 141:2

[5]See *Gleanings: Thoughts On Prayer* by Jennifer Kennedy Dean. "Principles of Receiving"

[6]Matthew 11:12; 12:28; Luke 17:20-21

[7]See *The Praying Life: Living Beyond Your Limits* by Jennifer Kennedy Dean (New Hope, Birmingham, AL, 1992) for a detailed treatment of the purpose of prayer.

[8]1 Kings 19:15; Psalm 19:1-4; Isaiah 6:3; 66:1

[9]Reprinted from *Prayer* by O. Hallesby, copyright 1931, Augsburg Publishing House. Used by permission of Augsburg Fortress.

All books referenced in this chapter can be ordered by using the order blank at the end of this book.

# 2

# Can You Know God's Will?

What is the key to consistently seeing God's power brought to earth through prayer? What is the key to power praying? The answer is found in 1 John 5:14-15. "This is the confidence we have in approaching God: that if we ask anything according to his will, he hears us. And if we know that he hears us—whatever we ask—we know that we have what we have asked of him." Do you see? We can have unwavering confidence that we have what we have asked for *when we know we are asking according to His will.*

The will of God is an area of struggle for most of us. The struggle takes two forms. (1) What if I don't like God's will? and (2) How can I know God's will? Let's examine each of these struggles.

## What If I Don't Like God's Will?

Human nature immediately responds to the above truth with disappointment. Human nature says: "But I was hoping to find out how to pray so that God would do my will, see things my way. What if I don't like God's will?" Often, when we hear the term "the will of God," our minds immediately turn to the least pleasant scenario. How often have you heard this thought expressed? "I was afraid that if I turned my life completely over to God, He'd make me go to deepest, darkest Africa."

Satan has a great deal invested in his propaganda campaign. His favorite slogan is: "God wants to deprive you. You can't be in God's will unless you're miserable and suffering." He feeds you that message in numerous subtle and not-so-subtle ways. It sounds true and reasonable.

For example, the world—Satan's sphere of influence—continually puts forth it's doctrine. We are bombarded with images telling us that happiness lies in externals—brighter teeth, shinier hair, more luxurious cars. The completion of that though is that internal, spiritual, invisible assets are worthless. If God calls on us to focus on and value His kingdom—internal, spiritual, invisible riches—He must be calling on us to sacrifice happiness.

Further, Satan's doctrine—disseminated through the world—tells us that joy and contentment are to be found in immediate self-gratification. The completion of this thought is that any activity that is other-centered or God-centered robs us of joy and contentment. If God calls on us to gratify ourselves by dying to ourselves, to find joy and contentment in Him, then He must be calling on us to be joyless and discontent.

Do you see how reasonable it sounds? Yet it is the farthest thing from the truth. In Romans 12: 2, God teaches us that His will is "good," which means *beneficial*, "pleasing," which means *pleasant or bringing pleasure*, and "perfect," which means *a perfect fit*. God's will is not something that is imposed upon you, but something that is built into you. Following God's will is following your own deepest longings. He has set eternity into the hearts of men (Ecc. 3:11), therefore only eternity satisfies the hearts of men.[1]

## God's Built-in Will

The will of God is encoded in His creation. The world exists because of His will. "For you created all things, and by your will they were created and have their being" (Rev. 4:11). Again we read in 1 Corinthians 8:6, "...God, the Father, from whom all things came...." All things exist because He wills them to exist. Creation working perfectly is the first expression of God's will.

As scientists discover more about the intricate workings of creation, we realize how perfect in every detail is the will of God. From the lowliest amoeba to the complex operation of the human body, every detail is flawlessly designed—an expression of the orderly, intentional mind of the Creator. In fact, the Greek word "cosmos," usually translated "world" or "earth," means *an orderly arrangement*. We learn the nature of God's will in the logical, practical, orderly way He put the world together.

Just as the Creator built His will into creation, He built His specific will for you into your being. When you are living in and praying in the will of God, you are living and praying the most authentic expression of yourself. His will is not a burden He is placing on you; but instead His will is your only freedom. He has created you to be an expression of His will.

> Therefore, I urge you, brothers, in view of God's mercy, to offer your bodies as living sacrifices, holy and pleasing to God—this is your spiritual act of worship. Do not conform any longer to the pattern of this world, but be transformed by the renewing of your mind. *Then you will be able to test and approve what God's will is—* his good, pleasing and perfect will (Rom. 12:1-2).

When we give ourselves completely to God, when our lives become an offering to Him, something happens. Our minds, our thinking patterns, are renewed. (We will address this process in greater detail in later chapters.) The result is that we will be able to prove the will of God by putting it to the test. We will try out (test) the will of God, made known to our renewed minds, and prove it to be good, acceptable and perfect. Our bodies will become the instruments through which He acts out His will. Our confidence will become like that of the psalmist when he wrote: "Your promises have been thoroughly tested, and your servant loves them" (Ps. 119:140).

When we have thoroughly tested God's will, spelled out in His promises, we will come to love His will. We will understand that His will is our good. Our praise to Him will become, "I delight to do your will, O God. Your laws are written in my heart" (Ps.40:8).

Recently I read an article in a news magazine about a political candidate who was recommending hard budget choices. The article referred to him as "the broccoli man" because, the writer explained, he's good for you, but you don't like him. I thought that an apt description of how we think of God's will. Somehow, deep inside, we know that God's will is best for us, but we assume it will be unpleasant. God's will is not something you have to bear up under, or endure gracefully, or settle for. God's will is a perfect fit.

Living outside of God's will is like having my foot squeezed into high-heeled, pointy toed shoes. They may be my shoe size. They may look good. They may match my outfit perfectly. They may have cost a fortune. But they pinch. If I were to compare the shape of my foot with the shape of that shoe, I would quickly see that my foot is not destined for that shoe. That shoe is not designed for my foot.

God's will does not pinch. The world squeezes you into a mold. The Spirit of God transforms you so that the outer you fits the inner you. When living out His will, you are wearing a destiny—a life-direction—that has been tailor-made for you.

If you were very wealthy, you could hire a clothing designer to design a wardrobe just for you. The purpose of each design would be to show you at your best. His thoughts would be focused on you. What colors will enhance your natural coloring? What styles will flatter you? You would be the designer's only concern.

God is the designer of your life. He has not designed a generic, off-the-rack plan that will fit just anybody. His will for you is created and planned *just for you.* He will "...instruct [you] the way chosen for [you]" (Ps. 25:12). He will "...instruct you and teach you the way you should go" (Ps. 32:8).

God's will harmonizes your life. God wills that your spirit, soul, and body live in concert rather than at odds. Paul defines the frustrations of living with spirit, soul, and body at cross-purposes in Romans 7:14-21.[2] He says that spirit, soul, and body wage war against one another—until one is completely surrendered to God's plan. God's plan, God's will, is that we live "...in accordance with the Spirit" (Rom. 8:5). Living in accordance with, or in harmony with, the Spirit means living in harmony with the true nature of things, since He is the Spirit of Truth and will lead us into all truth. Then what we have been seeking has found us. "The mind controlled by the Spirit is life and peace" (Rom. 8:6).

The will of God fuses the diverse aspects of your nature into a cooperating whole. No longer do you live the life of frustration and failure that results in doing what you don't want to do and not doing what you do want to do—your actions in conflict with your intentions.

As you begin to live and pray the will of God, you are aligning yourself with eternal realities. Remember that God created order out of chaos. He is the creator of "cosmos," orderly arrangement. You function most efficiently and productively within His will, in line with His plan for your life. "In him we live and move and have our being" (Acts 17:28). You are at home in Him.

**Practice Power Praying**

"'Your kingdom come, your will be done on earth, as it is in heaven'" (Matt. 6:10).

What is the specific prayer need in your life right now? What is your immediate, emotional, not logical, reaction when you apply Jesus' prayer to that need? How do you feel about the will of God when you put it in terms of your personal situation? Be completely honest about your answers.

Now, rethink your need. This time, ignore your ingrained and emotional reactions to the phrase "God's will." Think about God's will accurately, truthfully, according to His Word. Write down true words that define His will for your situation—words like "beneficial, pleasing, tailor-made, orderly."

Make this prayer your own:

Today's date _____

*Father,*

*I trust You. I know that Your plans are for good and not for harm. I know that You know the whole picture and are acting in accordance with it. I know that You only tear down in order to build up. I know that You only empty in order to fill. Let Your will be done.*

*In Jesus' Name.*

In every situation in your life, in the lives of people you love, God's will is a perfect fit. You can trust that when you pray "Let Your kingdom come in this life... in this situation... in this circumstance; let Your will be done in this life... in this situation... in this circumstance...," you are praying the very best result.[3]

## How Can I Know God's Will?

The rest of this book will deal with this question. In this section, I will introduce concepts that I will continue to clarify.

God's will is a mystery, but it is a mystery that He has revealed. In Colossians 1:25-26, Paul says that God had given him a commission "...to present to you the word of God in its fullness—

the mystery that has been kept hidden for ages and generations, but is now disclosed to the saints."

Time and time again, scripture refers to the mystery of His will, once hidden, but now revealed. In Romans, Paul talks about "the revelation of the mystery hidden for long ages past, but now revealed and made known through the prophetic writings by the command of the eternal God so that all nations might believe and obey him." (Rom. 16:25-26). The prophetic writings were in place, but the deep mystery of God's will contained in them has only been revealed since the Spirit came to indwell believers. The mystery of His will is now revealed.

God wants you to understand His will. He wants you to have *"the full riches of complete understanding."*[4] He has given His Spirit so that "we might *understand* what God has freely given us."[5] Jesus has come and "has given us *understanding* so that we might know him who is true."[6] He wants to "fill you with the knowledge of his will through all spiritual wisdom and understanding."[7]

Does it sound as if God is keeping His will a secret? On the contrary, He has made every provision for you to know His will. He wants you to know His will. He invites you to know His will. In fact, understanding His will is the cornerstone of power praying. You cannot pray with power if you do not pray according to His will. Since He designed prayer to be the conduit that brings His power to earth, and since He designs all things perfectly, He plans for you to know His will. He plans for prayer to work.

The path His will takes, the way He brings His will into being, remains a mystery. "Oh, the depth of the riches of the wisdom and knowledge of God! How unsearchable his judgments, and his paths beyond tracing out!" (Rom. 11:33). God will never hand over to us His all-knowingness. Sometimes we mistake His "will" for His "ways" and become confused. When I think that I have reached an understanding of God's will and begin to pray according to it, He often begins bringing His will about in a way that looks to me like a mistake. I have now built up enough history with Him that usually I know to wait and watch—not to confuse His ways with His will. I'm learning not to confuse *what* He's doing with *how* He's doing it.

## Joseph's Example

Consider the story of Joseph, which begins in the thirty-seventh chapter of Genesis and continues through the first chapter of Exodus.

24

What was God's will for Joseph? God showed Joseph His plan in a series of dreams. Joseph came to understand that he would be a ruler to whom even his father and brothers would bow. The next we hear of Joseph, he is at the bottom of a well listening to his brothers plot his death and begging for his life. He is sold into slavery, taken as a slave to a foreign land, and thrown into prison after being falsely accused. It does not appear that God is bringing about His will. It appears that God has lost control of Joseph's life because of the choices of evil men. Actually, God is working out His plan for Joseph so that He can work out His plan for Israel so that He can work out His plan for humanity.

For God's perspective on the situation, look at Psalm 105. What is God's will for Israel, the nation? Read verses 8-11. Summed up, it is this: "'To you I will give the land of Canaan as the portion you will inherit'" (v. 11). When Israel first reached Canaan, they were "but few in number, few indeed, and strangers in it. They wandered from nation to nation, from one kingdom to another" (vv.12-13). What did God need to do in order to bring His will about? He needed to give Israel a place to grow, prosper, learn skills, and reproduce safely. He needed to put them under the protection of a larger, more advanced civilization for a time. He needed them in Egypt.

How did He do it? "He sent a man before them—Joseph, sold as a slave" (Ps. 105:17). It looked as if Joseph's evil brothers had sent him to Egypt. It looked as if God's will was being thwarted by bad decisions. But God said that it was He who sent Joseph to Egypt. Joseph explained it to his brothers like this: "'But God sent me ahead of you to preserve for you a remnant on earth and to save your lives by a great deliverance. So then, it was not you who sent me here, but God'" (Gen. 45:7-8). God used seemingly adverse circumstances to position Joseph for receiving the promise.

How did God get Israel out of Canaan into Egypt? "He called down famine on the land and destroyed all their supplies of food" (v. 16). He brought famine on the land, but first He prepared their deliverance. It was waiting for them in Egypt. What appeared to be a disaster and a tragedy drove them to God's provision.

How was God bringing about His will for Joseph and at the same time bringing His plan for His people into being? God allowed Joseph to be put in a position from which God could display His power in just the way that would give Joseph the most credibility with the pharoah. "They bruised his feet with shackles, his neck was put in irons, till what he foretold came to pass, till the word of the Lord proved him true. The king sent and released him, the ruler of people set him free. He made him master of his household, ruler over all he possessed, to instruct his princes as he pleased and teach his elders wisdom" (vv. 18-11). Did God bring about exactly what He had promised Joseph He would do? Yes, to the last detail. Did God do it as Joseph expected Him to? No, far from it.

When God had Joseph in place, when He had brought about His plan for Joseph, His Joseph-plan could merge with His Israel-plan. Israel moved into Egypt under the protection of Joseph, whom God had put in place. In Egypt, the tiny nation of Israel grew to become a large nation. "Then Israel entered Egypt;...The Lord made his people very fruitful" (vv. 23-24).

Exodus chapter one tells us that the nation of Israel grew so large and so strong that it frightened the new king. "'Look,' he said to his people, 'the Israelites have become much too numerous for us. Come, we must deal shrewdly with them or they will become even more numerous and, if war breaks out, will join our enemies, fight against us and leave the country.' So they put slave masters over them to oppress them with forced labor..." (Ex. 1:8-11).

What was the next step in God's plan for His people? He wanted to toughen them up, physically, mentally and spiritually, and get them ready to take the land He had promised from their enemies. So what did He do? "The Lord made his people very fruitful; he made them too numerous for their foes, *whose hearts he turned* to hate his people, to conspire against his servants" (vv. 24-25). Do you see? It appeared that the Israelites became victims to the whim of the new pharoah. The truth is that God was moving Israel forward. He was engineering Israel's next step toward possessing the promise. What looked like a set-back was really a step forward. He had grown the nation of Israel in number. Now He wanted to grow them in character. When they were ready, He wanted them to possess the promise. He wanted to drive them out of Egypt, the land to which they had become accustomed, and propel them into the Land of the Promise.

God's plan was that Israel would be the channel for His will into all the nations of the earth. God's will is not short-term, but flows from generation to generation.

How God does His will is up to Him. You cannot control God or tell Him how to accomplish His plan. He will do His will in His way.

Oh, the depth of the riches of the wisdom and knowledge of God! How unsearchable his judgments, and his paths beyond tracing out. Who has known the mind of the Lord? Or who has been his counselor? (Rom. 11:33-34).

Does the clay say to the potter, 'What are you making?'...It is I who made the earth and created mankind upon it (Is. 45:9-12).

Who has understood the mind of the Lord, or instructed him as his counselor? Whom did the Lord consult to enlighten him, and who taught him the right way? (Is. 40:13-14).

When you treat prayer as if you have the right to tell God how to do His work, you will be disappointed. God does not take instructions. When you realize that God's ways are not your ways, that His ways are superior to your ways, you will not be thrown off balance when circumstances seem to be leading away from God's will rather than towards it. You can trust that God is steadily moving forward in the direction of His will.

**Practice Power Praying**

As you read through the story of Joseph, where did you identify? Did the Spirit clarify for you some circumstances in your life in which He is doing His will in His way, and you have been discouraged, thinking His will is not being done? Is it possible that your need or desire is wrapped up in God's bigger agenda, like Joseph's was? Make this prayer your own:

Today's date: _____

*Father,*

*I know that You are always working out Your perfect will in response to my prayers. I have surrendered my situation to You and I know You are moving it toward the best, most beneficial, long-term resolution. Your ways are higher than my ways.*

*In Jesus' Name*

"Prayer is none other than an act of the believer working together with God. Prayer is the union of the believer's thought with the will of God. The prayer which a believer utters on earth is but the voicing of the Lord's will in heaven....Prayer is the occasion wherein to express our desire for God's will. Prayer means that our will is standing on God's side. Aside from this, there is no such thing as prayer." (*Let Us Pray*, Watchman Nee)[8]

List current needs and desires. Beside each, write as much of God's will as you are certain about. Next, consciously align yourself with that will and speak it in prayer. For those aspects of the situation, the details, about which you do not know God's will for certain, pray for His will to be accomplished and His kingdom to be established. You do not have to know the specifics of God' will to pray God's will with great power. Pray about every detail of your situation in this way.

## God's Will Revealed

God wants you to know His will so that you can pray His will. Since He longs for your prayers more than you long to pray, isn't it sensible to believe that He has made and is making His will clear, not keeping it in the form of a riddle?

What He desires is specific for each situation and each life. Certain guiding principles are set forth that will always define His will, but He Himself will apply those principles and personalize them. He has a direct and tailored plan for you. Do not assume that God's plan for you is the same as God's plan for someone else. Do not define God's plan for now by God's plan for a previous time. God's plan is not stagnant. Instead, it is always unfolding and He is always revealing new twists and turns. "The path of the righteous is like the first gleam of dawn, shining ever brighter till the full light of day" (Prov. 4:18). In other words, God will be progressively making His will known, step by step.

Now the question arises: How can I learn to receive what God is revealing to me about His will? How can I understand the things of the Spirit?

[1]Psalm 103:5; Psalm 63:3-5

[2]See Gleanings: Thoughts on Prayer by Jennifer Kennedy Dean. "The Law of the Spirit"

[3]See The Praying Life: Living Beyond Your Limits by Jennifer Kennedy Dean (New Hope, Birmingham, AL, 1994), page 22 for further treatment of this topic.

# 3

# How Does Jesus Reveal God's Will to You?

God reveals Himself in three ways. He reveals His will through creation, through Jesus, and through scripture. In this and the following chapter we will closely examine each of these methods.

## God's Revelation Through Creation

Let me begin with how God reveals Himself through His creation. Romans 1:20 says, "Since the creation of the world God's invisible qualities—his eternal power and divine nature—have been clearly seen, being understood from what has been made...." Look carefully at what Paul said. The qualities of God that you cannot observe directly by using your physical senses can be observed in His creation.

"The heavens declare the glory of God; the skies proclaim the work of his hands. Day after day they pour forth speech; night after night they display knowledge. There is no speech or language where their voice is not heard. Their voice goes out into all the earth, their words to the ends of the world" (Ps. 19:1-4). To put it simply, creation is always talking about God.

This goes beyond the obvious fact that an observer of nature would have to reach the conclusion that a Creator exists. Paul says that the invisible qualities of God can be clearly seen and understood in His creation. It means that earth is a three-dimensional model of heaven.

By "earth," I mean planet earth, the physical creation, material and tangible aspects of life. By "heaven," I mean the spiritual realities of life. The two aspects of reality, heaven and earth, impact one another.[1] Earth is "what is seen" and heaven is "what is unseen" (2 Cor. 4:18). Heaven and earth— the seen and the unseen, or the material and the spiritual—are two ends of one continuum called "reality" or "truth."

Which existed first, physical reality or spiritual reality? Of course, spiritual reality existed first. The spiritual world had been in existence long before the material world was created by the Trinity. The spiritual world already had a history before earth came to be. Lucifer had already led his rebellion and been barred from God's throne room when planet earth and its inhabitants were spoken into being. The tabernacle existed in heaven before God told Moses to make a copy of it on the earth.[2] The Son existed in heaven before He existed on earth in material form.[3]

When God created the earth, He created a material model of the spiritual world already in existence. Earth is a picture of the spiritual realities that pre-existed it. Earth-reality was made out of spirit-reality. "By faith we understand that the universe was formed at God's command, so that *what is seen* was *not* made out *of what was visible*" (Heb. 11:3). To state it another way, *what we can see* was made out of *what we can't see*. Spiritual reality is always the causative agent of material reality.

Now that planet earth has been created, what holds it together? Hebrews 1:3 says "The Son is... sustaining all things by his powerful word." Spirit-force holds the earth and the universe together. Spirit-force—the Son's powerful Word—is the glue that sustains matter. "He is before all things and in him all things hold together" (Col. 1:17). Spirit-power—Jesus—is the lynchpin of creation.[4] Material reality, God's creation, does not function apart from God.

God's material creation is an allegory to illustrate spiritual reality. Jesus often pointed to earth to explain heaven. "Look at the grass... look at the birds of the air... look at the lilies of the field... look at the fields of wheat... look at the fig tree..." Earth is our visual. This fact has many applications, and we will explore it further when we talk about faith. For now, though, I want you to see that God has given us pictures of spiritual truth in His creation. The more we learn about creation, the more clearly we see the pictures. I will use many pictures from nature and science to show you ways that God has revealed Himself to us. These will all be allegories to which the scripture points us.

## God's Revelation Through Jesus

God has fully revealed Himself through Jesus. "The Word became flesh and made his dwelling among us" (John 1:14). In the first chapter of John, Jesus is called the Word. In the Greek, the word used is "logos." It means *the message, the full and meaningful expression of thought*. It means *a declaration*. I've always thought it was interesting that God called Jesus the Message instead of the Messenger. A messenger is separate from the message. Once a messenger has delivered the message, he is no longer relevant. However, Jesus is the Message. He always has been the Message and always will be the Message. Apart from the living Jesus, the mind, heart, and thoughts of God have no expression. They are inaccessible.

Suppose that you wanted to know my desires. In order for you to know my will or my desires, I would have to express my thoughts to you. Unless you know what I think, you cannot possibly know what I desire.

What would give you access to my thoughts? How could I put my thoughts into a form that makes them knowable? Words! When I express my thoughts in words, then my thoughts and my words are exactly the same thing. My words are the exact expression of my thoughts. If you want to know my thoughts, know my words. "In the beginning was the Word, and the Word was with God, and *the Word was God*" (John 1:1). God speaks to us only one way— by the Son, who is "...the exact representation of his being."[5] The Father and the Son are one, as certainly as my thoughts and my words are one.

God communicates His will through Jesus. Where is Jesus? Jesus is in heaven and on earth! His Life links the two ends of the continuum and brings heaven onto earth and earth into heaven.

## Jesus: The Expression of God's Desires

Jesus is in heaven. He is seated at the right hand of the Father in the heavenly realms as Paul states in Ephesians 1:20. Because I am in Him, I am seated at the right hand of God and am the recipient of every spiritual blessing heaven holds.[6] My life is hidden in His, Paul tells us in Colossians 3:3. Wherever Jesus is, I am. I am *in Him*. I am clothed with Him. His precious, perfect Life has become my covering because I have taken up residence in Him.

I believe that the following description would accurately depict the scene in heaven's throne room: Jesus, continual and perfect intercessor who intercedes only according to God's will, is before the Father. He is presenting His intercessions. Where am I, the intercessor on earth, in this scene? I am inside Jesus. Picture this. In the spiritual realm, I am presenting my petitions through His mouth. When I pray, my words reach the Father's ears through the Son.

In the material realm, on earth, He is living *in me*. Jesus is in me and the Father is in Jesus. The Father is the Thought Who expresses Himself through the Word. Jesus is the Word Who expresses Himself through me. "I in them and you in me" (John 17:23). In John 15, Jesus tells me that His Life will flow through me like the vine's life flows through the branch. This is a fact woven through the entire New Covenant: Christ is in me. I no longer live, but Christ lives in me.

For the transactions of faith that occur in the earth end of the continuum, He has clothed Himself in me. He expresses His power through me. He expresses His Life through my earth-body. My body becomes the vehicle through which He does His work. Prayer from the earth-view looks like this: I am praying. Where is Jesus in this scene? He is *in me*. He is speaking through my mouth. His thoughts are in my mind; His words are in my mouth; His desires are in my heart.

In both ends of the continuum, Jesus is the power. I am always expressing Him. In both realities, I in Him and He in me, He is the Life. His Life is the animating force in both settings. When we pray, both scenes are occurring simultaneously. Jesus' Life brings the spirit realm into the earth realm and the earth realm into the spirit realm.

The Word of God, the expression of His heart and will, is a living Person whose Life is my life. God continues to speak His Word through Jesus. In order to understand the Father's revelation of His will, I have to trust the present-tense Life of the Living Jesus in me, and my present-tense life in the Living Jesus.[7]

## Practice Power Praying

"Delight yourself in the Lord and he will give you the desires of your heart" (Ps. 37:4).

The word "delight" comes from a Hebrew word that means *soft, moldable or pliable*. To delight in the Lord means to be pliable in His hands and to be molded by Him. He will mold your desires so that they match His will. He will give you the desires of your heart.

The world "heart" would be more accurately translated "mind." When God has access to a willing mind, that mind becomes the tablet upon which He inscribes His desires.

Are you moldable in His hands? Are you delighting yourself in Him?[8]

**Make this prayer your own:**

Today's date _____

*Father:*

*Teach me what it means to delight myself in You. I want to be moldable in Your hands. Create my desires.*

*In Jesus' Name.*

"In its simplest analysis prayer—all prayer—has, must have, two parts. First, a God to give....And just as certainly there must be a second factor, *a man to receive*. Man's willingness is God's channel to the earth...Let it be said that God can do nothing for the man with shut hand and shut life. There must be an open hand and heart and life *through* which God can give what He longs to. An open life, an open hand, open upward, is the pipe line of communication between the heart of God and this old befooled world. Our prayer is God's opportunity to get into the world that would shut Him out." *(Quiet Talks on Prayer*, S.D. Gordon)[9]

List your needs. Beside each of your prayer needs, write this commitment: "In this circumstance, I want to receive what You want to give. My hand, heart, and life are open to You."

## God is Speaking Through Jesus Now

God did not quit speaking when the Bible was finished. He didn't say all He had to say and then stop. I DO NOT MEAN THAT THE BIBLE IS ANYTHING LESS THAN THE AUTHORITATIVE COMPLETE WORD OF GOD. I mean that the Father continues to speak the scripture in the present tense.

Several words for "word" or "speak" are used in the New Testament. One word is "laleo." This word means *the act of speaking.* The content of what is said is not important. It means *to speak as opposed to being silent.* The word "laleo"is used in Hebrews 1:1-2: "In the past God spoke to our forefathers through the prophets at many times and in various ways, but in these last days he has spoken to us by his Son...." Here the scripture is saying that God has never been silent but has always been speaking. His speaking once occurred through the mouths of prophets, but now His speaking is through His Son. He has always been speaking and is now speaking.

The next word is "logos," at which we have already briefly looked. In "logos," the important factor is the content of what is being said. "Logos," from which comes the word "logic," is *the full expression of a logical thought.* Jesus is the "logos" of God. He is the full expression of God. Who He is and Who God is are the same thing. Jesus fully and accurately expressed the Father—made Him known. "No one has ever seen God, but God the One and Only, who is at the Father's side, has made him known" (John 1:18).

The third word is the word "rhema." "Rhema" means *the present-tense voicing of words.* The primary factor is voice or speaking. "Rhema" is *the word now being spoken.* When you read this book, you will be reading my "logos." But if I come to your area and teach this book to you myself, you will be hearing my "rhema." The content will not be different, but if you and I could sit down face to face, I could take the message of this book and apply it specifically to your life. That's what makes it "rhema." I speak it to you.

The word "rhema," then, refers to the fact that the Trinity, Elohim, is speaking the "logos" to me and it is becoming "rhema." The word "rhema" is used in Hebrews 1:3: "The Son is the radiance of God's glory and the exact representation of his being, sustaining all things by his powerful word." The word "rhema" is also used in Ephesians 6:17 in which Paul tells us that one of our spiritual weapons is "...the sword of the Spirit, which is the word of God." As the Father speaks His Word directly to me, I hold in my spirit-hand the weapon that will defeat the enemy—the speaking word of the Most High God, Creator of Heaven and Earth.

Do you see that it is the Life of Jesus operating at full power in me that communicates God's will? Jesus is the way God speaks. How do I speak? Through my mouth. How does God speak? Through Jesus. When I speak, what comes out of my mouth? Words. When God speaks, what comes out of His mouth? Jesus.

He is the Word of God in its every form. Jesus is the "laleo" and the "logos" and the "rhema." His Life is operating in me.

## The Life

For a period of time His Life was contained in an earth-body that God had prepared for Him. "'But a body you prepared for me...'" (Heb. 10:2b). His Life was something separate from His body, but was contained in and expressed through His body. During that period of time His work was limited to that one and only physical vehicle. When that earth-vehicle was destroyed, the Life it contained was no longer limited to one body. The Life that once was contained in the earth-body that was born in Bethlehem and died on a cross outside Jerusalem is now in my body and in your body and in the body of each believer. Now His Life operates on earth through my earth-body. When Jesus finished with His earth-body, the way was opened for His Life, His Spirit, to indwell the earth-bodies of His followers.

God shows us this truth in a picture He placed on the earth. Every object in the temple was a shadow or copy of a solid reality that exists in the spiritual realm. The writer of Hebrews explains that Jesus' earth-body was the reality pictured by the temple veil that hid the direct and immediate presence of God: "...a new and living way opened for us through the curtain, that is, His body" (Heb. 10:20).

When the real veil, His body, was destroyed, the shadow veil was also destroyed. "And when Jesus had cried out again in a loud voice, He gave up His spirit. At that moment the curtain of the temple was torn in two from top to bottom" (Matt. 25:50-51). The presence of God—His Spirit, His Life—was no longer contained in a place or in a single earth-body. His presence became accessible to anyone who would enter through the new and living way, Jesus.

Now Jesus is in me. What is Jesus doing right now? Right now, Jesus is praying the will of the Father. Through me, on earth, He is praying the will of the Father. Through Him, in heaven, I am praying the will of the Father. His Life in me is creating desires that match God's will. "It is God who works in you to will...his good purpose" (Phil. 2:13). He is expressing His desires through my desires so that when I ask whatever I will, I am asking according to His will. He is causing my will to come into alignment with His. To know God's will so that I will know how to pray with power, I must trust His Life operating in me. His Life—His thoughts, His desires, His wisdom and understanding— is being expressed through a vehicle I call Jennifer.

## The Life Operating in Me

Let's look at how God speaks through His creation to explain the Life of Christ operating in me, expressing the Father's will.

A thread runs through the Bible from beginning to end, first page to last. The thread is blood. It first appears in the early chapters of Genesis when God slays animals to make coverings for Adam and Eve, and it is the central theme of the final book of Revelation. Surely blood is essential to our understanding of the spiritual end of the continuum.

Blood is an earth-substance that God gave us to illustrate a spiritual reality. Earth-blood is a copy or shadow of what blood means in heaven. God points us to this illustration in His creation by saying, "'For the life of a creature is in the blood...the life of every creature is its blood'" (Lev. 17:11 and 14). Do you see? Blood is the material illustration of a spiritual reality called "life."

"Life" is an intangible. Who can adequately define "life"? A body contains life one moment, and the next moment life is gone. Yet life is the central component of the Bible's message. God, when He was creating the material expression of spiritual reality, created blood as the earth-picture of Life. Blood, we will see, is not a death-picture, but a life-picture.

"'For the life of a creature is in the blood, and I have given it to you to make atonement for yourselves on the altar; it is the blood that makes atonement for one's life'" (Lev. 17:11).

>Where is a creature's life? *In its blood.*
>Why did God give us blood? *To make atonement on the altar.*
>What is it that makes atonement? *Blood.*
>What needs to be atoned? *One's life.*
>Why does blood make atonement? *Because it is the life.*
>What has the true value— the red sticky earth-stuff called blood, or the life the blood represents? *The life.*

Only life makes atonement for one's life. Without the shedding of blood, or the pouring out of life, there is no atonement, or putting away of sins. Do you see that God's Word has pointed us to an earth-picture to explain a spirit-truth? Let's closely examine this visual illustration and glean from it all the insight we can. Earth-blood is a parable of what blood means in heaven. Earth-blood is what God uses to stand for and picture LIFE.[10]

In your earth-body, is it not literally true that your life is in your blood? Without blood, there is no life. Your bloodstream is the delivery system for everything your body needs in order to thrive. Your bloodstream carries the nutrients and the oxygen your cells need. Your bloodstream washes away the toxins your cells release. You might say that as your blood flows through your body, old things are passing away and new things are coming. You might say that as your blood flows through your body, it is purifying you from all toxins. Your life is in your blood. Blood = Life.

The Spirit-breathed Word of God teaches us that in the spiritual realm there is only one Life. His name is Jesus. "'I am the...life'" (John 14:6). "In him was life..." (John 1:4). Life is only to be found in the Son. "He who has the Son has life; he who does not have the Son of God does not have life" (1 John 5:12). Life does not exist except in Him. Everything else that passes for life in the earth realm is really death in disguise. Why? Because at its outset it has only one possible outcome—death. Existence outside Jesus is a steady march toward death. Only through Him can we "[pass] from death to life" (1 John 3:14).

Why is the blood of Jesus so precious? Because it is His Life. It is His Life that imparts the value to His blood. Because not one drop of sin's infection invaded His Life, His blood was deemed pure.

Jesus' blood has two roles in our salvation:

(1) His earth-blood that He spilled out on the cross for payment of sin: "We were reconciled to him through the death of his Son..." (Rom. 5:10).

(2) His Spirit-blood, His Life, that He poured out before the Father in the heavenly tabernacle and His Spirit-blood that runs through your spirit-veins: "How much more, having been reconciled, shall we be *saved through his life!*" (Rom. 5:10).

His blood represents His death, which paid for our sins. His blood also represents His Life, which brings us continual salvation and deliverance. We are reconciled through His death, but we are saved by His Life.

Hebrews 9:11-12 tells us that Jesus, after shedding His earth-blood on the cross, went into the heavenly tabernacle to sprinkle His blood on the mercy seat and to pour that blood out before the Father.[11] He entered the Most Holy Place "by his own blood" instead of by the blood of goats and calves as had the earthly priests.

Consider this: Did Jesus go back down to earth and scoop up the red sticky earth-stuff called blood and bring it into the true tabernacle? Of course not. He did not take the picture; He took the substance. He did not pour out His earth-blood in the Most Holy Place. He poured out His Life—the Life that had met and conquered sin; the Life that had mastered death; the Life that had fulfilled the requirements for righteousness.

His earth-blood flowed through an earth-body and was subject to earthly limitations. The earth-blood He poured out at the cross soaked into the ground, coagulated, and degraded. It was made of earth-stuff.

His spirit-blood has no earthly limitations. His spirit-blood is Spirit-Life. The power of the Father flows through the Life of the Son. The fullness of God is in Jesus. (Col. 1:19) Just like earth-blood is the delivery system for everything your body needs to thrive, so the Life of the Son is the delivery system for everything you need to thrive spiritually. "His divine power has given us everything we need for life and godliness through our knowledge of him who called us by his own glory and excellence" (2 Peter 1:3).

Jesus Himself lives in and through me. His Life flows through me like blood flows through my body. The scripture says, "The blood of Jesus, his Son, purifies us from all sin" (1 John 1:7b). How does blood purify? It purifies from the inside. Blood does not cleanse by being applied externally. It cleanses only as it flows through. As blood flows through my body, its red cells absorb toxins and transport them to the organs through which they will be expelled. My blood cleanses me continually as it flows through me.

The Life of Jesus, Jesus Himself, flows through me like blood flows through my body. His blood in spirit form flows from heaven's mercy seat through me. "On that day a fountain will be opened to the house of David and the inhabitants of Jerusalem, to cleanse them from sin and impurity" (Zech. 13:1). Jesus' blood became a flowing fountain rather than a stagnant pool. The fountain of His blood flows through you and me to cleanse us from sin and impurity and to bring us perpetual newness of Life. The ever-flowing blood of Jesus is the delivery system for God's power. The power works in the blood.

## New Life Replaces Old Life

Look again at the picture on earth. How is your earth-blood manufactured? It is manufactured in your bone marrow. Hebrews 4:12 points us to the picture of bone marrow to represent spirit.[12]

Your bone is made of a porous material. A cross section of your bone would reveal that it has a cavity filled with a spongy substance called marrow. Veins run from the marrow through the pores in your bones into your blood stream. Blood cells are manufactured in your bone marrow. When they are mature, they move through the veins, and enter the bloodstream.

Your life, also called your blood, is continually being recreated. As one blood cell is used up, a new blood cell takes its place. In a sense, you are always in the process of being newly made. You are always becoming a new creation.

My bone marrow manufactures only my life. My bone marrow only manufactures blood cells with my DNA code in them. My bone marrow will never make anything except Jennifer-life. If you drew blood from me today and again three months from now, you would be drawing completely different blood cells. Yet they would all have exactly the same DNA code. Each blood cell, subjected to DNA testing, would be identified as Jennifer-life. My bone marrow will never manufacture anyone else's life.

The only way for my bone marrow to stop manufacturing Jennifer-life and start manufacturing some other kind of life would be for me to die and be born again. In the material realm, it cannot happen.

In the spiritual realm, this is exactly what happens. When I show up on planet earth, my spiritual marrow is manufacturing life with Adam DNA in it. My spirit cannot manufacture anything but Adam-life. Nothing I can do will make my spirit manufacture any other kind of life.

When I enter into Jesus, His Life becomes my life. I die to my Adam heritage, bury it, and am resurrected—born again in spirit—to live a new life. Not an improved version of my old life, but an altogether new Life, the Life of Jesus.[13]

What kind of life is Jesus? He is Eternal Life. John talks about "the eternal life, which was with the Father and has appeared to us" (1 John 1:2). "He is...eternal life" (1 John 5:20). He does not make my life eternal. He replaces my life with His Life and His Life is eternal.

What does the word "eternal" mean? It means having no beginning and having no ending. Eternal Life has always been and always will be. One occurrence in His eternal Life is His death and resurrection. When I enter into Him, I possess His eternal Life, which includes His death and His resurrection. If His Life is mine, then so is His death and so is His resurrection.[14]

When I enter into Him, I die to my Adam nature and live by my new Jesus nature. My spirit-marrow no longer manufactures Adam-life because that "I" has died. I have been born again, this time of the Spirit of God. Now my spirit-marrow manufactures Jesus-Life. In Galations 2:20, Paul says, "I have been crucified with Christ and I no longer live." In other words, *"My spirit-marrow no longer manufactures Adam-life because the Adam-offspring named Paul died with Christ."* Then Paul goes on to say, "...but Christ lives in me. The life I live in the body, I live by faith in the Son of God, who loved me and gave himself for me." In other words, *"I have been given a brand new spiritual DNA structure. I have become a completely new creation. My spirit-marrow now manufactures only Jesus-Life. The Life that flows through me is Jesus."*

## Progressively Made New

It seems, sometimes, that I am continuing to manufacture Adam-life even though I have been born again of the Spirit and have the Life of Jesus flowing through me. Is it that way with you? Perhaps you're thinking, " Why do I continue to sin if I no longer manufacture Adam-life in my spirit-marrow? Where do my sins come from?"

The way physical blood operates in our earth-bodies continues to be the visual representation of an invisible truth. Blood cells are continually being used up and replaced by new, fresh blood cells. Old blood cells are always passing away. New blood cells are always being created.

Old, residual Adam-life is still flowing through your spirit-veins. You are not manufacturing it anymore, but it has not all been sloughed away. However, as it is progressively eliminated, cell by cell, it is replaced with Jesus-Life. You are "being transformed into his likeness with ever-increasing glory, which comes from the Lord, who is the Spirit" (2 Cor. 3:18).

It seems that some people have a faster spiritual metabolism than others. Some people, it seems, progress quickly while others seem to make little or no progress. You can increase your spiritual metabolic rate the same way that scientists tell us we can increase our physical metabolic rate.

(1) Proper nutrition: Feed on the Word of God.(Jer. 15:16)
(2) Oxygenate your cells by deep breathing: Pray without ceasing. (1 Thess. 5:17)
(3) Exercise: Live by faith. (Col. 2:6)
(4) Drink plenty of water: Be continually filled with the Spirit. (John 7:37-39)

## The Life of Jesus Creates My Desires

Since the Life of Jesus is flowing through me and recreating me, I can trust Him to use my mind, my imagination, my desires, my understanding and intellect as conduits through which to express the will of God. I want to pray according to God's will so that my prayers will have power and effect. What is my first clue about God's will? My desires! Jesus said, "If My Life is flowing through you like the vine's life flows through the branch, then ask whatever you wish and it will be given you."[15] God is speaking to you in the Son. The Son is living His Life in you.

## His Eternal Life is My Confidence Before God

In 1 John 5:11-15 we read:

> And this is the testimony: God has given us eternal life, and this life is in his Son. He who has the Son has life; he who does not have the Son of God does not have life. I write these things to you who believe in the name of the Son of God so that you may know that you have eternal life. This is the confidence we have in approaching God: that if we ask anything according to his will he hears us. And if we know that he hears us— whatever we ask— we know that we have what we asked of him.

Take this passage apart and examine it with me.
**"God has given us eternal life..."**
*God has given us a new kind of life, Spirit-Life operating in an earth-body. This new kind of life is called "eternal life."*
**"...and this life is in his Son..."**
*This Life that God has given us is found in only one place: Jesus. Eternal Life is the Life of Jesus that God has transfused into us.*

**"He who has the Son has life..."**
*Jesus' Life is actively flowing through us like blood is actively flowing through our bodies. Jesus' Blood = Jesus' Life*
**"...he who does not have the Son of God does not have life."**
*Eternal Life only flows through the Son. Only those who have the Son have Life.*
**"I write these things to you who believe in the name of the Son of God so that you may know that you have eternal life."**
*These truths are written down so that you and I can be confident that the Son's Life flows through us— so that we can believe in the present-tense Life of Jesus operating in us. This is called "eternal life."*
**"This is the confidence we have in approaching God: that if we ask anything according to his will, he hears us. And if we know that he hears us—whatever we ask—we know that we have what we asked of him."**
*When the Life of Jesus is operating in me at full power, I can know the will of God and pray with confidence. His Life is my confidence.*

## Practice Power Praying

Picture your spirit-veins flowing with Jesus' blood. Feel His cleansing Life. Imagine His thoughts flowing into your mind and becoming your thoughts. Imagine His desires flowing into your heart and becoming your desires.

**Make this prayer your own:**
Today's date _____

*Father,*
*Thank you for giving me Life in Your Son. I believe Your promise that His present-tense Life is operating in me. I can know You. I can know Your heart and Your mind. I trust Your ability to speak to me. I lay my heart and my mind before You. Write Your will on them and make it mine.*
*In Jesus' name*

Begin now to operate in the reality of His Life in you. Your body is His vehicle. Your mind is His tablet.

## The Foundation of All Power Praying

What does the Life of Jesus flowing through me have to do with power praying? His present-tense Life active in me is how the Father communicates His will to me, teaches me to pray with power. Through The Life, God's power flows through me and is released onto the earth when I pray. God—Father, Son and Spirit—indwells me and displays Himself through me.

The Life of the Father flows through the Son.

"For God was pleased to have all his fullness dwell in him..." (Col. 1:19).

"...the Father, *from* whom all things came...Jesus Christ, *through* whom all things came..." (1 Cor. 8:6).

The Life of the Son flows through the Spirit.

"'All that belongs to the Father is mine. ...The Spirit will take from what is mine and make it known to you'" (John: 14-15).

*(The Spirit makes Jesus experientially known from within. He causes the indwelling Life of Jesus to be real in your experience.)*

The Life of the Spirit flows through me.

"'If anyone is thirsty, let him come to me and drink. Whoever believes in me,...streams of living water will flow from within him.' By this he meant the Spirit" (John 7:37-39).

*(The Life of Jesus will flow onto the earth from within believers by means of the Spirit.)*

| IF: | THEN: |
|---|---|
| The Life of the Father flows through the Son. | The Life of God flows through me. |
| The Life of the Son flows through the Spirit. | |
| The Life of the Spirit flows through me. | |

OR

| IF: | THEN: |
|---|---|
| Jesus expresses the Father. | I express God. |
| The Spirit expresses Jesus. | |
| I express the Spirit. | |

However you state it, it boils down to this: the Trinity is One, and Elohim, the Three-in-One God, lives in me and lives His Life through me. Jesus said, referring to those who will believe Him and obey Him,"'...*we* will come to him and make *our* home *in him*'" (John 14:23). His power is working within me (Eph. 3:20) and He is able and willing to put His thoughts into my mind, His Words into my mouth, His desires into my will, His emotions into my heart.

## His Faith Operates in Me

Paul said, "The life I live in the body, I live by faith in the Son of God" (Gal. 2:20). This, he had previously explained, was because his old nature—his Adam heritage—was dead and buried and Jesus was the only Life in him.

If I express Jesus' Life, then the faith that operates in me is Jesus' faith. Remember, I don't have any life, therefore any faith, of my own. The phrase translated "faith in the Son of God" might more accurately be translated "the faith which is in the Son of God."[16] The faith that flows through Jesus flows through me. If I'll let Him, He'll express His perfect, unshakable, mature faith through this Jennifer-vehicle.

He is everything for my praying life. It all depends on Him. Apart from Him, I can do nothing. I have nothing to offer, except His Life in me. I do not even have my own faith. I have His faith. His faith moves mountains.

[1]The word "heaven" is used in scripture in three different contexts. Sometimes "heaven" means the physical structures in the sky, such as in Psalm 19. Sometimes "heaven" means our spiritual dwelling place after physical death, such as it is described in the book of Revelation. But most often the word "heaven," "heavenlies," "heavenly places" refers to present-tense spiritual realities and spirit-beings that impact our lives. Heaven and earth are actually two ends of the same continuum.

[2]Hebrews 8:5; Exodous 25:40

[3]John 1:1-3; John 17:5

[4]Some years ago, scientists believed that matter was solid and static. That was before the discovery of the true structure of the atom. Actually, matter is made of up billions and billions of tiny, microscopic solar systems called atoms. An atom is in constant motion. In each atom, electrons orbit around a nucleus. The nucleus is made up of protons and neutrons strongly bound together. When the atom is split, the incredible force that binds the protons and neutrons together is released and we have atomic energy. So, when matter is reduced to its smallest element, an atom, and that atom is split, what remains? Pure energy—power. What is the power that holds the atom's nucleus together—the power that is released when it is split? What is the power that binds atom to atom? No one knows. But the scripture says that **Jesus holds the universe together with His powerful Spirit-word.**

[5]Hebrews 1:1-3

[6]Eph. 1:3; 2:5-6

[7]"On the first day of Pentecost He returned, not this time to be *with them* externally... but now to be *in them*, imparting *to them* His own divine nature, clothing Himself with *their* humanity.... He spoke with their lips, He worked with their hands. This was the miracle of new birth, and this remains the very heart of the Gospel!

"To be *in Christ*—that makes you fit for heaven; but for Christ to be *in you*—that makes you fit for earth! To be *in Christ*—that changes your destination; but for Christ to be *in you*—that changes your destiny! The one makes heaven your home—the other makes the world His workshop."

*The Saving Life of Christ*, Major W. Ian Thomas, (Zondervan Publishing House, Grand Rapids, MI, 1961), pp. 14-15, 19. Used by permission of Zondervan Publishing House.

[8]For a fuller treatment on this topic, see *Heart's Cry* by Jennifer Kennedy Dean, chapter one.

[9]S.D. Gordon, *Quiet Talks on Prayer* (Barbour and Company, Inc., Uhrichsville, OH, 1984), p. 12.

[10]For further treatment of this thought, see:

Jennifer Kennedy Dean, *Heart's Cry: Principles of Prayer* (New Hope, Birmingham, AL, 1992), pp. 10-17.

and

Dr. Paul Brand & Phillip Yancey, *In His Image* (Zondervan Publishing House, Grand Rapids, MI, 1984), pp. 51-80.

[11]In Hebrews 9:11-12, Jesus is portrayed as the high priest entering into the Most Holy Place by means of blood. Although this scripture reference does not specifically say that Jesus sprinkled His blood on the heavenly mercy seat and poured it out on the altar of burnt offering, we know that He did. The Jewish audience to which this epistle is written would have understood that His actions had been mirrored for generations by earthly high priests on the Day of Atonement. In Matthew 26:28 Jesus states, "'This is my blood of the covenant, which is poured out for many for the forgiveness of sins.'"

[12]"For the word of God...penetrates even to dividing soul and spirit, joints and marrow" (Heb. 4:12).

[13]Romans 6:1-10

[14]Romans 6:5-10; See also *Handbook to Happiness* by Charles R. Solomon (Tyndale House, Wheaton, IL, 1971), pages 66-71, for further treatment of this thought.

[15]My paraphrase of John 15:7.

[16]See *Word Pictures in the New Testament*, Vol. IV by A.T. Robertson (The Sunday School Board of the Southern Baptist Convention, 1931), p. 290.

and

Vincent's *Word Studies of the New Testament*, Vol. IV by Marvin R. Vincent (Hendrickson Publishers, Peabody, MS), p. 108.

Many of the books referenced in this chapter can be ordered by using the order form at the end of this book.

# 4

# How Does God Reveal His Will
# to You Through His Word?

Clearly understanding that Jesus' Life is flowing through you and operating in you is essential for understanding everything else about prayer. His Life is the underlying reality, the ground from which every prayer principle grows.

Jesus taught us that His Spirit-Life in us would be superior to His physical presence with us. He said to His disciples, who had grown dependent upon His earthly presence, "'I tell you the truth: It is *for your good* that I am going away. Unless I go away, the Counselor will not come to you; but if I go, I will send him to you'" (John 16:7). Jesus said that His Life indwelling us in Spirit-form would be to our benefit. Why? Because from within, Jesus Himself would speak directly into our understanding. We can hear Him more clearly than the disciples could hear Him when He was on earth in physical form. We can hear with understanding. We can hear His "rhema," His present-tense speaking, all the time. He never leaves us. This form of hearing— hearing from within, Spirit-voice to spirit-ears— is superior to hearing with our earth-ears. Spirit-hearing is more reliable than earth-hearing. Jesus said it is *for our benefit* that He has made His Spirit-Life available and has removed His physical presence.[1]

Depend on His Life flowing through you right now. Depend on His Spirit-voice speaking to your understanding. Any understanding about spiritual truth that you acquire comes directly from Him. He may use a tool— a teacher, a writer, a preacher— but that person is a tool, not a source. He is the one and only source of spiritual understanding. Trust Him. He speaks by opening your mind so that you can understand the scripture. (See Luke 24:14.)

## God's Word Working

God does His work by His Word. When God speaks, His Word is the instrument of His work.

> As the rain and snow come down from heaven, and do not return to it without watering the earth and making it bud and flourish, so that it yields seed for the sower and bread for the eater, so is my word that goes out from my mouth: It will not return to me empty, but will accomplish what I desire and achieve the purpose for which I sent it (Is. 55:10-11).

Do you see how God talks about His Word? He says that He sends His Word out with an assignment and that His Word always accomplishes His desires and achieves His purposes. His Word accomplishes His work. His Word waters and nourishes the lives into which He sends it and makes them bud and flourish. He always does His work by His Word.

> By the word of the Lord were the heavens made, their starry host by the breath of his mouth....
> For he spoke and it came to be; he commanded and it stood firm (Ps. 33:6 and 9).

Jesus once said, "'The *words* I say to you are not just my own. Rather, it is the Father, living in me, who is doing his *work*'" (John 14:10). Jesus said that the words He was speaking were doing the Father's work. Why? Because they were the Father's Words! The Father's Words do the Father's work.

In the same passage, Jesus continued by saying, "'Believe me when I say that I am in the Father and the Father is in me; or at least believe on the evidence of the miracles themselves'"(John 14:11). Here's what Jesus was saying: *The Father's Words, which I am speaking, are doing the Father's miracles. Here's the proof that the Father is in Me: His Words coming through Me are doing His works.*

God's Words are different from your words or my words. In the material realm, words have no substance. They do not have mass and take up space. They are puffs of air. Earth-words communicate, but they do not accomplish work. I can't say to an object, "Move from here to there," and expect the object to move. I have to use physical force to move an earth-object from one place to another. My words do not do my work.

The Father's Words are different. In the spiritual realm, God's Words have substance. They are not puffs of air; they are the instruments of His action."God said, 'Let there be light,' and there was light" (Gen. 1:3). He created the earth by His Word. He is watching over His Word to see that it is carried out.

## Spirit-words Doing Spirit-work

His Words are spirit. Jesus, whose words were the Father's, said, "The words I have spoken to you are spirit and they are life" (John 6:63). Spirit, remember, is the cause of the material realm and is the genesis of activity on the earth. Earth is the reflection or the shadow of activity occurring in the spiritual realm.

For example, Paul teaches us in Ephesians 6:12 that our enemies are not flesh and blood. Rather, they are powers and principalities in the heavenly realms. It would appear that flesh and blood, people, are standing in the way of God's purposes. But scripture tells us that what we see on the earth is the result of what is happening in the heavenly realms. We also learn that the remedy for what is happening on earth will be accomplished in the spiritual realm. Victories in the spiritual realm result in changes in the physical realm. Earth is subject to the powers of Spirit.

God's Word, a Spirit-force, does God's Spirit-work. When God's Spirit-work is done, it is reflected on the earth. God's Word created the earth and God's Word sustains the earth. The created is subject to and dependent upon the Creator. The created is physical, but the Creator is Spirit. The material realm is subject to the spiritual realm.

## God's Spirit-words Spoken on Earth

Remember this about the physical Jesus, Jesus in His earth-body: the physical Jesus was the beginning of a new lineage. He is called the last Adam.[2]

The first Adam was created in the image of God, so he was spirit. He was packaged in a body made out of earth-stuff. He was a spirit-man packaged in an earth-body. However, when He chose to disobey God, his spirit-nature died. He became an earth-man in an earth-body.

The last Adam was born of a woman named Mary, an earth-person, and the Spirit of God. When conception takes place in the physical realm, the genetic material of the father and the genetic material of the mother merge to make a brand new person. The man Jesus was the combination of God's Life, which is Spirit, and Mary's life, which is flesh. He was a Spirit-man in an earth-body.

Every person since Adam has been the spiritual offspring of Adam—until Jesus. In Jesus, God started over. Once again, a Spirit-man lived in the earth environment. His flesh, or His human nature, was subjected to every fleshly pull. He was fully exposed to the power of sin. He engaged Satan in hand-to-hand combat on Satan's turf—and won! This time, Spirit subjugated flesh. This time Spirit perfected flesh. When He had become perfect— when His Spirit-nature had won every battle with His flesh-nature and had emerged the victor— then He could become the source of salvation for everyone who believes.[3] He could be the progenitor of a whole new race—Spirit-men in earth-bodies.[4] He became the first-born among many offspring, the firstfruit of a full harvest. You and I can be born again, this time of the Spirit. We can have Jesus' Life operating in our earth-bodies. We can live the same Life and Power on earth that Jesus did.

## The Power of His Present-tense Life

You and I are to live Spirit-Life in earth-bodies just like the physical Jesus did. "'I tell you the truth, anyone who has faith in me will do what I have been doing. He will do even greater things than these, because I am going to my Father'"(John 14:12). Do you understand what Jesus said? He said that His followers can live in the physical environment called earth in the same way that He did. Why? Because He was going to the Father. His physical presence would be removed and replaced by His Spirit presence within. This would enable His followers to do the same things He did—on a greater scale. The word "greater" here means quantitatively greater, not qualitatively. Because He would not be limited to one earth-body, but would indwell the earth-bodies of all believers, He would do even more mighty works because He had more bodies through whom to do these works.

When Jesus said that He spoke the Father's words, that means that you and I can speak the Father's words. When Jesus said that the Father living in Him did His work, that means that the Father living in me will do His work. When Jesus said that the words He spoke were spirit, that means that I, too, can speak words that are spirit.

How do I speak words that are spirit? "This is what we speak, not in words taught us by human wisdom, but in words taught by the Spirit, expressing spiritual truths in *spiritual words*" (1 Cor. 2:13). Let's examine this passage in 1 Corinthians 2:9-13 to see how we reach the point of speaking spirit-words:

**"'No eye has seen, no ear has heard, no mind has conceived what God has prepared for those who love him'..."**

*God has things prepared for us—things that are ready and waiting for our use. We cannot know these things in the same way we know what exists on the earth. We can't know God's provision by seeing or hearing or imagining.*

**"...but God has revealed them to us by his Spirit."**

*What we cannot know by seeing, hearing or imagining, we can know by the Spirit's revelation. The word "revelation" means uncovering or unveiling. The Spirit unveils God's truths to our understanding. When the Spirit brings understanding, we will know what God has ready and waiting as certainly as if we'd seen them with our eyes or heard them with our ears.*

**"The Spirit searches everything, even the deep things of God."**

*When we are depending on the Spirit to bring understanding of spiritual truth, we will have access to even the deep, mysterious, hidden things that belong to God.*

**"For who among man knows the thoughts of a man except the spirit of the man within him?"**

*No one knows me but me. No one knows my thoughts but my spirit within me. If you want to know what I think, I will have to reveal my thoughts to you.*

**"In the same way, no one knows the thoughts of God except the Spirit of God."**

*Just like no one knows me but me, no one knows God but God. If you want to know His thoughts, He will have to reveal them to you.*

**"We have been given not the spirit of the world, but the Spirit who is from God that we might understand what God has freely given us."**

*God has revealed Himself to us. He has given us His Spirit. He has given us Himself. The purpose for giving us His Spirit is so that we can understand what He has prepared for us and has made freely available to us.*

**"This is what we speak, not in words taught by human wisdom, but in words taught by the Spirit, expressing spiritual truths in spiritual words."**

*What do we speak? We speak what we understand. What does God's Spirit cause us to understand? From the Spirit, we understand what God has freely given us. If God Himself has revealed truth into our understanding, when we speak that understanding, we are speaking spiritual words. What makes them spiritual? They are born of the Spirit. Whatever is born of the Spirit is Spirit. We can now say, "These words I speak, they are spirit and they are life."*

In prayer, we speak the things that we know by the Spirit to be freely available to us. These words are spirit and life. They are God's Words. God's Words do exactly what God has assigned them to do. They are settled forever in the heavens. God's Words do God's work. Spirit-force—God's Word—produces power on the earth. He is watching to see that *His Word* is carried out. Powerful and effective prayer is God's Word spoken in prayer.

When I speak God's Words on earth, they impact the spiritual realm. The spiritual realm impacts the material realm. The Life of Jesus flowing through me continually is creating my thoughts, desires, imaginings, and will, and is authoring in me the Spirit-Word of God.

## Practice Power Praying

Pray with an awareness that you are praying God's Word. Consider the fact that He has authored in you His desires. You are speaking the will of God into the spiritual realm. You are praying from a position of strength. You are making known to the powers and principalities in heavenly realms what the manifold wisdom of God is (Eph. 3:10). You are speaking in the name of Jesus and at His name every knee has to bow and every tongue has to admit that He is Lord.

Examine this passage in Philippians 2:9-11.

"God exalted him to the highest place and gave him the name that is above every name," Paul writes. Is this present-tense truth, or future-tense truth? Is Jesus already exalted to the highest place? Is He already the name above every name?[5] Paul has described finished work—a work that is completed and available in the spiritual realm, or the "heavenlies."

What is God's reason for exalting Jesus and giving Him the name above all names? The scripture says it is so that "at the name of Jesus every knee should bow, *in heaven* and *on earth* and *under the earth*, and every tongue confess that Jesus Christ is Lord to the glory of God the Father." Is this present-tense truth, or future-tense truth? It is present tense! It is true now and will continue to be true throughout eternity. Right now, at the name of Jesus, every knee in the spiritual realm bows and every tongue in the spiritual realm has to admit the Lordship of Jesus and become subject to the authority of Jesus.[6]

**Make this prayer your own:**

Today's date _____

*In the name of Jesus, I declare the mighty, active and living Word of God. In the name of Jesus, I declare victory in every challenge. I declare supply for every need. At the name of Jesus, in the spiritual realm, every spiritual force becomes subject to His authority.*

## The Words of God Recorded in the Scripture

All scripture is given by inspiration of God. Every word written in the book called the Bible is the Word of God. God spoke it through the Bible's authors and speaks it continually through His Spirit to you and to me. God takes the scriptures and makes them present-tense. Without the Spirit, they are words on a page bound in a book. The Spirit makes the words of scripture alive and active. The words of scripture are not  merely a historical report, but are a summons in which words written down in the past become contemporary. They carry a power that is working in the present.

As the Spirit of God, God within you, reveals the deep and hidden truths, His Word becomes the mold in which your prayers are shaped. Jesus said, "If you remain in my word and my words remain in you, ask whatever you wish and it will be given you" (John 15:7). The Word of God becomes so strongly entrenched in your life that it forms an outgoing current called prayer.

In order to give the Spirit plenty of material to work with, you need to continually put the Word of God on deposit in your life. Proverbs 2:1 tells you to store up His commands within yourself. As you commit yourself to the daily discipline of taking in the Word of God, He will begin making it alive within you. When you put the Word on deposit, He can make withdrawals at opportune times.

In Mark 4:2-8, Jesus tells a parable that uses the earth-picture of seed to demonstrate the Spirit-truth about the Word of God. A seed will remain a seed, will produce nothing, until it is placed into a nurturing environment. The environment needed by the Word of God is the human heart, or mind. Once the seed is planted, it produces fruit. Once the Word is stored up, put on deposit, or planted in your mind, it will bear fruit.

This parable goes on to say that some seed "'...grew and produced a crop, multiplying thirty, sixty, or even a hundred times'" (Mark 4:8). Ask the Lord for a hundred-fold increase. Ask Him to bring forth a full and running-over crop of wisdom and insight.

Scripture also pictures the Word of God as nourishment for your spirit in the same way that food is nourishment for your body.[7]

> How sweet are your promises to my taste, sweeter than honey to my mouth! (Ps. 119:103).

> Then he said to me, 'Son of man, eat this scroll I am giving you and fill your stomach with it.' So I ate it, and it tasted as sweet as honey in my mouth (Ez. 3:3).

> When your words came, I ate them; they were my joy and my heart's delight (Jer. 15:16).

> Jesus answered, 'It is written: "Man does not live on bread alone, but on every word that comes from the mouth of God'(Matt. 4:4).

A consistent intake of God's Word will nourish and strengthen your spiritual immune system, produce spiritual growth, increase spiritual strength, and enhance spiritual alertness. Feeding on the Word of God is essential for power praying.

What we eat literally enters into and becomes part of what we are. The nutrients are extracted from the food and delivered to the cells by means of the bloodstream. When you "eat" the Word of God, you provide the Spirit with the opportunity to deliver power to your life by means of the flowing Life of Christ.

## The Foundation of God's Will in His Law

One aspect of God's Word is His law, or His commandments and statutes. In His law we clearly encounter His will. God as law-giver is frequently misrepresented.

One can view a law-giver from two perspectives: First, there's the overbearing, power-hungry, demanding authority figure who says, "I'm laying down the law and you have to obey it because I'm the one with the power. I'm establishing a code of behavior that suits me, and I'm expecting you to follow my rules. If you don't, I'll punish you."

This is not God the law-giver.

Here's God the law-giver: "I'm the Creator. I made everything that exists. Because I love you, I'm giving you the laws of the universe. I'm telling you how to get the most out of all that I have created for you. I'm telling you the secrets about how things work so that you can live the life you are created for."

God is the law-giver because God is the Creator.

God's will for you is that you flourish and prosper. His law is your protection and your wisdom. His law is encoded in your spiritual DNA so that in following it you are cooperating in establishing your own fulfillment and success.

DNA is another earth-picture that explains spirit-truth. Your DNA is the instruction manual for your body. It tells each cell how to do its job. Everything about your physical structure is encoded in your DNA. Your DNA determines what size shoe you'll wear, what color your hair or eyes will be, how tall you'll grow. You will be unable to change anything prescribed by your DNA because it is structural. You can make cosmetic changes, but not structural ones. For example, you can dye your hair, but it will always grow out the color your DNA says it is.

God's law is encoded in your spiritual DNA. It is written in your heart. You cannot change it. He has built His law into the structure of human beings. In working against it, we are working against our own best interest. In resisting it, we resist peace and harmony. Outside His law, we are engaged in an ongoing, energy-draining, life-sapping upstream swim. In giving us His law, He has not restricted us, but freed us.

> I run in the path of your commands, for you have set my heart free....Direct me in the path or your commands, for there I find delight (Ps. 119:32, 35).

> The law of the Lord is perfect, reviving the soul....The precepts of the Lord are right, giving joy to the heart (Ps. 19:7-8).

## God's Will is Progressively Made Plain

Think of God's will as a journey. He is progressively revealing His will. The starting point is His law.

When I have appointments that will require that I drive during rush hour, I always listen to the traffic reports. I have a destination firmly in mind, and I want to avoid any situation that will entangle me and slow my progress. I want to reach my destination with the least amount of resistance. God's law is like a traffic report on your journey. He shows you what to avoid and what alternate routes to take to avoid anything that will impede your progress.

His plan is something that flows through your life from beginning to end. Actually, His will transcends the days of your earth-life. His will for you was in process before you were born and will continue to flow from your life into the lives of generations to come. "But the plans of the Lord stand firm forever; the purpose of his heart through all generations" (Ps. 33:11).

Obeying His commands is the first step of the journey deep into His will. The more clearly you understand His will, the more powerfully you will pray.

## Practice
## Power
## Praying

The psalmist writes of God's laws: "By them is your servant warned; in keeping them there is great reward" (Ps. 19:11).

Do you see any areas of your life in which you are ignoring God's precepts? If so, do you realize that you are diminishing your life and diluting the power of your prayers?

Do you see that willful sin will eventually enslave you? "Keep your servant also from willful sins; may they not rule over me" (Ps. 19:13). "Direct my footsteps according to your word; let no sin rule over me" (Ps. 119:133).

Do you realize that disobedience will impair your spiritual senses by which you discern God's will?

**Make this prayer your own:**

Today's date:_____

*Father,*

*I open my life to You. Search me, know my thoughts. Try me, know my ways. Show me any wrong direction in my life. Put my feet back on Your path. I will settle for nothing less than all You have for me. Therefore, I forsake every wrong way. Lead me in the everlasting way. "I open my mouth and pant, longing for your commands" (Ps. 119:131).*

*In Jesus' name.*

Let the Spirit of Truth guide you into all Truth. Let your sin come into contact with God's grace. Let Him set you free.

[1]For a full explanation of how the Spirit speaks from within, see *The Praying Life: Living Beyond Your Limits* by Jennifer Kennedy Dean, pp. 38-48.

[2]1 Corinthians 15:45. See also Romans 6:14. Adam was a pattern of Christ.

[3]Hebrews 5:8-9

[4]Hebrews 2:10-13; Romans 8:29

[5]Ephesians 1:20-21

[6]The phrase "should bow" does not mean "ought to bow." The word "should" means *implying necessity in accordance with the nature of things or with the divine appointment and therefore certain, destined to take place.* At the name of Jesus, it is necessary in accordance with the nature of things—it is certain to take place— every knee bows and tongue confesses His lordship. It is a present-tense reality in the spiritual realm—the name of Jesus stops the forces of Satan cold.

[7]For an extended treatment of this concept, see *The Praying Life: Living Beyond Your Limits* by Jennifer Kennedy Dean, pp. 50-52.

Any of the books referenced in this chapter can be ordered by using the order blank at the end of this book.

# 5

# How Does God Reveal His Will To You Through Spiritual Vision?

God intends for you to know, understand and be filled with His will so that you will have confidence in prayer, knowing how to make full use of the power of prayer. How will you know the nuances of God's will along with those aspects of His will clearly written in scripture?

Paul says this: "I pray that *the eyes of your heart may be enlightened* in order that you may *know* the hope to which he has called you, the riches of his glorious inheritance in the saints, and his incomparably great power for us who believe" (Eph. 1:18-19). God wants to *show* you His will. He wants your inner eyes to receive light so that you will *know*. The Greek word translated "know" in this passage literally means *to see; not the mere act of seeing but the actual perception of some object; to see and understand.* This particular Greek word suggests fullness of knowledge, not progressing or growing in knowledge. To know in this sense means to fully understand. God's plan is that we will see the hope, the riches, and the power.

"I see!" You've probably used these words to mean, "I understand fully!" God wants you to see the hope of your calling, the riches available to you, and His incomparably great power for you. Jesus said to Nicodemus, "'I tell you the truth, no one can see the kingdom of God unless he is born again'" (John 3:3). To state it another way, if a person is born again, he can see the kingdom of God. The person whom the Spirit of God indwells has the spiritual

61

ability to see. Seeing spirit-truth changes one's perception of material facts.

Here's what I mean: Jesus suggested to Nicodemus that the Spirit is like the wind. Once again, Jesus points to an earth-picture to explain a spirit-truth. The wind has no substance. You don't know where it comes from or where its going. You can't grab hold of it and feel its texture. You only know wind because of its effects.

Suppose, then, that a person decides that he does not believe in the wind. Wind, he decides, is the figment of someone's imagination. No one can prove wind. He prefers to stick to things that can be empirically proven. This person will reach some strange conclusions about what is true. For example, this person will conclude that trees lean over all by themselves sometimes; or that leaves lying quietly on the ground sometimes jump up and twirl through the air. This person will ascribe power where there is no power. He will not understand that the trees and the leaves are responding to a power that is acting on them.

If a person who does not believe in the wind and a person who believes in and understands the wind look at the same scene, they will see two startlingly different truths. The first will see trees bending over, the second will see the wind.

The person who learns to observe with spirit-eyes will look at earth and see Spirit. This person will understand that everything he sees on the earth is the effect of spirit. This person will know and understand the whole truth, the reality, and will not be limited to time-bound, earth-bound perceptions and short-sighted vision. This person, seeing the truth, will be free to live in harmony with it, no longer bound to and limited by a caricature of the truth. Jesus said, "'If you hold to my teaching, you are really my disciples. Then you will know the truth, and *the truth will set you free'*" (John 8:31).

## See the Kingdom

Jesus uses the language of "seeing" when He explains how He knew God's will while limited to His earth-abilities. He said, "'I tell you the truth, the Son can do nothing by himself; he can do only what he *sees* his Father doing, because whatever the Father does, the Son also does. For the Father loves the Son and *shows* him all he does'" (John 5:19-20). Another time He stated, "'I am telling you what I have *seen* in the Father's presence'"(John 8:38). When Jesus makes these statements, He is not talking about what

He saw in His pre-existent state, when He was with the Father before He came to earth. When Jesus came to earth, He took upon Himself the form of a man. In other words, He limited Himself to living in time and space. He has no access to pre-existent knowledge.

God gives His children spiritual vision. In order to understand how spiritual vision functions, we'll look at physical vision.

What is "vision"? Vision is the ability to see. What I *see* becomes what I *know*. For example, once I see the color red, I know what the color red looks like. Once I see a person's face, I know what that person looks like. Everything I see becomes part of what I know.

What I see gives me direction. I have to see where I'm going in order to get to my destination. I need physical vision to navigate my physical world.

However, I don't see with my eyes. I see with my brain. My eyeballs receive the stimuli, reflected light, which is carried as electrical impulses to my brain. When the electrical impulses reach my occipital lobe, an image registers on my brain. My brain interprets it, decides on the proper response, stamps it into my memory and processes it into everything else that I know. "Seeing" is a finished work when my brain has developed a picture and has given it what we call "meaning."

The brain's ability to see can be activated by the imagination or the memory. Your brain can picture a familiar scene or can create a scene out of random information stored in your memory bank.

"Seeing" is when a picture is imprinted on your brain and has become part of what you know.

Vision differs from the other physical senses. To use any of the other senses, you need only two things: the stimulus and the ability to receive the stimulus. In other words, to hear you need something to hear and the ability to hear it; to taste you need something to taste and the ability to taste it. Each sense works this way—except the sense of sight. Sight requires the presence of a third element. In order to see, you need something to see, the ability to see it, and LIGHT. Vision occurs when your eyes receive the light reflected off an object and send the image to your brain. Without the presence of light, vision cannot occur.

Spiritual vision works the same way. Spiritual vision occurs when God creates a picture within your mind—on your brain— of spiritual realities. In physical vision, the impetus for sight is light bouncing off physical objects. In spiritual vision, the impetus for sight is light reflected off spiritual realities. Vision cannot occur without a light source. The Light Source for spiritual vision is Jesus.

The Jesus-Light illuminates kingdom realities. They register on my understanding and become part of what I know. Remember Paul's prayer? "I pray that the eyes of your heart will be enlightened so that you will *know...*" (Eph. 1:17).

Solid, true, authentic kingdom realities are within you. When you were born into the kingdom of God the kingdom of God was born into you. Kingdom realities are within you and "the true light that gives light to every man,"[1] Jesus, is causing you to "see" them. They are imprinted on your brain. You understand them.

How will you know the hope to which He has called you? How will you know His riches which He has invested in you? How will you know His incomparably great power that is working for you and in you? He will give you Light. He will enlighten the eyes of your heart. Then you will know. You will see and fully perceive.

Through the steady discipline of prayer, spiritual vision is sharpened. The more we live in His presence, the more opportunity He has to enhance our ability to see and bring into sharper focus what we already see.

### Spiritual Vision Surpasses Physical Vision

The person with clear spiritual vision will recognize dimensions of reality that are invisible to the physical senses. In the second chapter of Luke we are introduced to two such people.

"Now there was a man in Jerusalem called Simeon, who was righteous and devout. He was waiting for the consolation of Israel, and the Holy Spirit was upon him. It had been revealed to him by the Holy Spirit that he would not die before he had seen the Lord's Christ" (Luke 2:25-26). What have we learned about Simeon so far? We know that he has no distinctive titles or holds no position of leadership. He is described merely as a man in Jerusalem. We know that the Holy Spirit was upon him. In other words, he was especially attuned to the movings of the Spirit and his life was open and available for the Spirit's leadings. We know that God had placed into Simeon's life a vision— a clear mental picture of a future event. The vision is a promise from God. The Spirit had revealed to Simeon that he would not die until he had seen the Messiah.

In the verses 27 through 28 we read, "Moved by the Spirit, he went into the temple courts. When the parents brought in the child Jesus to do for him what the custom of the law required, Simeon took him in his arms and praised God, saying: 'Sovereign Lord, as you have promised, you now dismiss your servant in peace. For my eyes have seen your salvation.'" Now we see that Simeon, moving in the flow of the Spirit, went to the temple where he saw Mary and Joseph bringing the infant Jesus "to do for him what the custom of the law required." Do you see what that phrase implies? Mary and Joseph were doing something ordinary—something every Jewish family did. Probably other families were doing the same thing on the same day. Yet when Simeon looked at this ordinary, everyday scene, he saw what no one else saw. He saw the Messiah when everybody else saw a mother and a father and a baby. Others saw the appearance. Simeon saw the Truth.

Next we meet a woman named Anna. In Luke 2:36-38 we learn that Anna was a prophetess. She was especially called and gifted by God to discern His activity in the world. She had spent most of her life worshiping, fasting, and praying. In prayer, she had developed an extreme sensitivity to the moving of the Spirit. Like Simeon, when she looked at the family from Nazareth she recognized the Messiah, the Promise of God.

Nothing in the material realm identified Jesus as God's Promised One. Only those who had spiritual vision recognized Him. Those who knew the scriptures and the law best, the religious leaders of the day, did not recognize the Truth when He stood in front of them. Jesus said they were "blind guides." Their spiritual eyes were darkened, and they did not see the Spirit. Their understanding was limited to things they could perceive with their physical senses.

## Spiritual Vision Works Two Ways

In Simeon, we can clearly see vision working in two ways. One, God gave him a specific promise upon which Simeon could base his prayers. God showed Simeon through His Spirit that Simeon would see the Messiah before he died. The scripture says it had been revealed to him. This wording implies that the promise did not come in a sudden one-time encounter, but progressively took root in his understanding as he lived in the anointing of the Spirit. The idea grew in him and took on substance until he knew it with certainty. He saw it. It became part of what he knew.

The second way we can see vision working is in Simeon's ability to see the Spirit in an ordinary event. When he looked at earth, he saw spirit-truth—he saw the Wind. He was alert to the Spirit. He expected the promise. Spiritual vision gives the ability to discern between appearance and truth. We will discuss this concept in more depth in Chapter 6.

Over and over again we see in the scripture that God works by first implanting vision. Abraham, Noah, Moses, Gideon, Paul, Jesus... the list goes on. God implants vision. God nurtures vision. God causes vision to become reality on the earth.

## God Implants Vision

Vision is Spirit-work. Only God can put truth in you and make it vision. Truth, when it is external, is an idea or a belief. It only becomes vision when it is within you. Like a baby grows inside a woman's body until time for it to be born onto the earth, vision grows in the spirit of a believer until the time for it to become reality on the earth.

When God brought forth on the earth His ultimate Promise, He did so by means of pregnancy and birth. Again, we can see an earth-picture that teaches a spirit-principle. God will impregnate you with vision. He will put vision *in you* to bring it forth *through you* to change the world *around you.*

Vision will first appear in your life in embryonic form. Vision does not come into your life full-grown. It will need time to gestate. God initiates the vision. You will need to provide the vision with the proper conditions for maturing.

**The vision needs a spirit-womb.** Your innermost being available to God's powerful work is the place where the vision grows. Your Spirit-filled life is the environment in which the vision develops.

**The vision needs nourishment.** Feed the vision the Word of God. As you fill your life with God's Word, the vision will grow stronger and healthier. It will take on clearer focus, become more substantive. The natural result of nourishing your spirit will be that the vision God has entrusted to you will mature.

**The vision has developmental stages.** Be patient. God always reveals His infinite truth in finite stages. The vision will progressively unfold as you walk in obedience. Consider Abraham. Observe how his vision continued to unfold and develop.

In Genesis 12:1-4, God first implants the vision. "The Lord had said to Abram, 'Leave your country, your people and your father's household and go to the land I will show you. I will make you into a great nation and I will bless you; I will make your name great and you will be a blessing. I will bless those who bless you, and whoever curses you I will curse; and all peoples on earth will be blessed through you.' So Abraham left, as the Lord had told him...."

The vision was vague at best. Abraham is to go to a land that God will show him. God will bless him and make him into a great nation. Abraham knows no more than that. He has no clear picture of the mature plan, just an embryonic vision. But he left, as the Lord had told him.

When Abraham reaches a certain place in Canaan, the Lord appears to him. This time He was a little more specific. "To your offspring I will give this land," He said in Genesis 12:7. The vision was taking clearer shape. It had moved from "a land I'll show you" to "this land."

In chapter 13, verse 14, Abraham has given the vision time and nourishment, and God fleshes it out further. "'Lift up your eyes from where you are and look north and south, east and west. All the land that you see I will give to you and your offspring forever. I will make your offspring like the dust of the earth, so that if anyone could count the dust, then your offspring could be counted. Go, walk through the length and breadth of the land, for I am giving it to you.'" God lays out the boundaries of the land. Furthermore, He expands on His promise to make of Abraham a great nation. He clarifies that the vision is not only qualitative greatness, but numerical greatness.

Abraham has a problem—at least he thinks he does. God has given him the vision of fathering a great nation, but Abraham doesn't even have one son. Abraham expresses his concern. "'O Sovereign Lord, what can you give me since I remain childless and the one who will inherit my estate is Eliezer of Damascus?...You have given me no children; so a servant in my household will be my heir'" (Gen. 15:2-3). Notice how Abraham states his analysis. He says, "You *have given* me no children... a servant *will be* my heir." Abraham thinks it's too late. He sees only one way for God to bring the vision about: He'll have to use Abraham's servant, Eliezer of Damascus. In response, God gives Abraham more detail of the vision, a detail He had not yet stated. "'This man will not be your heir, but a son coming from your own body will be your heir.'" The vision continues to take on clearer form.

In Genesis 15:13-16, God fills in more details. For the first time He tells Abraham that his descendants will be strangers in a country that will enslave them for four hundred years, but afterward they will come out with great possessions. In the fourth generation, God says, Abraham's descendants will return to the Promised Land. Then, in verse 18, God adds more specifics. He gives clearer boundaries of the land of the vision. "'To your descendants I give this land, from the river of Egypt to the great river, the Euphrates— the land of the Kenites, Kenizzites, Kadmonites, Hitties, Perizzites, Rephaites, Amorites, Canaanites, Girgashites and Jebusites.'" The vision has progressed from "the land I'll show you," to "this land" to the detailed description above. Progressive vision. Each step of obedience opening up new dimensions, new understandings. One step makes the next step clear. Step by step, Abraham follows the Voice that grows the vision.

Finally, God appears to Abraham when he is 99 years old. In the physical realm, Abraham still has no heir. Yet God says, "'No longer will you be called Abram; your name will be Abraham, for I have made you a father of many nations'"(Gen. 17:5). Do you see what God said? "I *have made you* a father of many nations." Before that, God had said "I *will make you* a father of many nations." In the spiritual realm, the work is done. The only thing left is for spiritual truth to be manifested in the material realm. In verses 6-14, God sets forth the terms of the covenant. He gives Abraham a sign of the covenant in the flesh—circumcision. He tells Abraham clearly that not only will the heir come from his own body, but from the body of his wife Sarah. He says, "'My covenant I will establish with Isaac, whom Sarah will bear to you this time next year'" (Gen. 17:21). Now the vision is full-term. It is ready to be born on the earth.

**The vision has a due date.** The vision is for an appointed time. God implanted it in your life at exactly the right time and He will bring it about at exactly the right time. My tendency is to try to induce labor as soon as the vision enters my life. I'm inclined to be impatient. It always looks like the right time to me. God is teaching me to wait for the due date. When the vision has reached the right developmental stage, nothing can hold it back. Until that time, nothing can bring it forth.

**The vision is God's, not yours.** You are only hosting the vision. He has placed His vision into your imagination, creativity, understanding, and desires. He will bring about His vision. "'Surely, as I have planned, so it will be, and as I have purposed, so it will stand'" (Is. 14:24).

## Spiritual Vision Brings Spiritual Understanding

He creates in you an understanding of circumstances in your life from His perspective. You can learn to look at each situation as it is on earth and see the situation as it will be when brought into contact with God's power.

Earth-perspective gives only a vague outline, affords only a linear perspective. The earth point of view is like an artist's ebauche. An ebauche is the initial underpainting that establishes the broad lines of emphasis in a projected painting. It is unfinished. The ebauche is never meant to be the finished work. If you were to mistake an artist's ebauche for his finished work, you would misjudge his talent. If you did not wait for the mature and finished work—if you walked away having seen only the ebauche—you would never truly see the painting. The finished work exists in the mind of the artist.

When you are using your spiritual vision, God will show you the finished work before it becomes available on the earth. It is already finished in His mind. Your spirit-eyes will see it before your earth-eyes do. You will distinguish between an ebauche and a finished work of art.

For example, in 2 Chronicles 20:1-2, scripture first defines the earth-view of Judah's situation, the ebauche. "The Moabites and Ammonites with some of the Meunites came to make war on Jehosophat. Some men came and told Jehosophat, 'A vast army is coming against you from Edom and from the other side of the Sea. It is already in Hazazon Tamar.'" Jehosophat, however, understood that this dire description of the facts did not constitute the whole of reality. "Jehosophat resolved to inquire of the Lord, and he proclaimed a fast for all Judah" (v. 3).

God began to fill Jehosophat's mind with His greatness. "'O Lord, God of our fathers, are you not the God who is in heaven? You rule over all the kingdoms of the nations. Power and might are in your hand, and no one can withstand you...'"(vv. 6-12). With every statement God's Spirit prompted in Jehosophat, his spiritual vision sharpened. He began to see the situation as it would be. God announced it to him through the mouth of the prophet Jahaziel: "'Do not be afraid or discouraged because of this vast army. For the battle is not yours, but God's. Tomorrow march down against them.... You will not have to fight this battle. Take up your positions; stand firm and see the deliverance the Lord will give you'" (vv.15-17). Before this picture was finished on earth, it was finished in the spiritual realm. The situation on earth merely laid out the broad lines of emphasis where the power of God would be directly applied. Spiritual vision enables you to see that what God has promised He is bringing to pass. He "...calls things that are not as though they were" (Rom. 4:17).

## Practice Power Praying

What impossible situation confronts you at this moment? How does it look from the earth perspective? You do not have to deny the negative in order to pray with power. You simply have to view the situation in the light of kingdom realities.

Look at Abraham's example. He fully faced the situation, but also fully embraced the vision.

Against all hope, Abraham in hope believed and so became the father of many nations, just as it had been said to him, 'So shall your offspring be.' Without weakening in his faith, he faced the fact that his body was as good as dead— since he was about a hundred years old— and that Sarah's womb was also dead. Yet he did not waiver through unbelief regarding the promise of God, but was strengthened in his faith and gave glory to God, being fully persuaded that God had power to do what he had promised (Rom. 4:18-21).

Look fearlessly and realistically at your situation. Don't let the circumstances intimidate you out of trusting the vision. Abraham *believed* and so *became*. Place your circumstances against the backdrop of God's promises. Let God recreate your perspective. What do you see in the presence of your Father?

## The Purpose of Spiritual Vision

Why does God do His work through vision? Why engage humans before the fact? Why not just let His work show up on earth unannounced? God says, "'See the former things have taken place, and new things I declare; Before they spring into being I announce them to you'" (Is. 42:9). He announces His intentions into our desires or understanding; then He brings His intentions into being in response to our prayers. Why?

In Isaiah 48:3-6 we read, "'I foretold the former things long ago, my mouth announced them and I made them known; then suddenly I acted, and they came to pass. For I knew how stubborn you were; the sinews of your neck were iron, your forehead was bronze. Therefore I told you these things long ago; before they happened I announced them to you so that you could not say, 'My idols did them; my wooden image and metal god ordained them.'" In other words, God will announce His plans before He brings them into being so that we will recognize His work and will not attribute His power to anyone or anything else.

Jesus said, "'I have told you now before it happens, so that when it does happen, you will believe'" (John 14:30). When you see the picture inside you take shape on the earth you will recognize the work of the One who has the power to do what He has promised (Rom. 4:21).

God gives impossible vision. If it were possible, it would be an assignment or a project—but it is vision. When vision takes shape on the earth, there will be no doubt about Whose vision it is. God will implant vision in you that only He can bring into being. "We have these treasures in jars of clay so that we will know that this all-surpassing power is from him and not from us" (2 Cor. 4:7).

If you have scaled back or watered down God's vision, you are not "[taking] hold of that for which Christ Jesus took hold of [you]" (Phil. 3:12b). God will not bring about a diluted form of His vision. You may bring about a diluted form of His vision, but He will not. If what you are envisioning about a situation negates or underestimates the power of God, you are not praying the vision, not claiming the promise. You are limiting God by expecting of Him only what you can imagine.

What do you see in the presence of your Father?

## Practice Power Praying

"And so after waiting patiently, Abraham received what was promised" (Heb. 6:15).

List each of your concerns or needs that are pointing you to God's supply. To the best of your ability to discern spiritual truth, what is God causing you to envision about His power applied to your situation? Define for yourself the "ebauche." Then define the finished work in God's mind.

As you do this, remember that we all feel somewhat insecure about our ability to discern God's voice. We are all progressing in our ability to use our spiritual senses. With practice, you will become more certain. Don't let your insecurity defeat you. Leave it to God to teach and correct. Start where you are.

**Make this prayer your own:**

Today's date: _____

*Father,*

*I am insecure about my ability to hear, but I am confident about Your ability to speak. I trust You to make Your message clear. You have promised to do whatever is necessary to reach me. I trust You.*

*In Jesus' name.*

Now let the Father speak this promise to you: "I will go before you and will level the mountains; I will break down gates of bronze and cut through bars of iron. I will give you the treasures of darkness, riches stored in secret places, *so that you may know that I am the Lord, the God of Israel, who summons you by name*" (Is. 45:2-3).

¹John 1:9

# 6

# How Does Faith Bring the Vision Into Being on the Earth?

How does vision become reality on the earth? How does the picture God has placed within you take shape in the material realm?

"The promise *(vision)* comes *(takes shape in the material realm)* by faith" (Rom. 4:16). Faith is the midwife of vision. Prayer is spoken faith. Examine this statement that Paul made in the book of Romans:

**"The promise comes..."**
*Comes from where to where? From heaven to earth.*
**"The promise comes..."**
*How? What is the avenue that brings the promise from heaven to earth?*
**"The promise comes by faith."**
*Faith brings the promise out of heaven and makes it reality on the earth.*

## What Is Faith?
The scripture gives us numerous descriptions of faith. It tells what faith is and what faith is not. We will look at several of these. The scripture says that faith *is*:

    (1) A life. (Heb. 10:38)
    (2) The substance of things hoped for. (Heb. 11:1, KJV)
    (3) The evidence of things not seen. (Heb. 11:1, KJV)

The scripture says that faith is *not*:

    (1) Sight. (2 Cor. 5:7)
    (2) Work. (Heb. 4:10; Rom. 4:4-5)

## The Life of Faith

"My righteous one will live by faith" (Heb. 10:38). Faith is not a feeling you are required to stir up. Faith is not a static attendance to a set of theological beliefs. Faith is not something you get out and dust off when you want something from God. Faith is a way of living. Until it becomes a way of living, it will not be effective. **Faith is obeying the present-tense voice of the Father.** Faith is not believing something; faith is **believing Someone.**

Faith is not just how you deal with certain promises, but a continual interaction with the spiritual realm. Think of faith as a spiritual organ through which you receive and use spiritual resources. In the earth-realm, for example, your eyes are the organ through which you receive light. Light is pressing in around you, but your eyes have to be open to receive it. Your lungs are the organ through which you receive oxygen. Oxygen is pressing in around you, but your lungs have to function in order to take it in. The spirit-resources of heaven are available and pressing in around you, but you must live by faith in order to receive and use them.

You already have access to the eternal resources of God, the spiritual aspects of reality. Faith is how you take them into your life and use them. God's promises are not for someday, they're for today.

> For he *has rescued* us from the dominion of darkness and *brought us* into the kingdom of the Son he loves (Col. 1:13).

> Praise be to the God and Father of our Lord Jesus Christ, who *has blessed* us in the heavenly realms with every spiritual blessing in Christ (Eph. 1:3).

> And God *raised us up* with Christ and *seated us* with him in the heavenly realms in Christ Jesus (Eph. 2:6).

> For you died, and your life *is now hidden* with Christ in God (Col. 3:3).

When God's Word speaks of the spiritual world, of the resources of Christ, the action is spoken of as already completed. Faith brings the available resources of God into our lives. The promise comes by faith.

Suppose someone handed me a check for $1,000,000. Would I then be a millionaire? No—I would have a check for $1,000,000, but I would not have $1,000,000. I would not become a millionaire until I cashed the check and transferred money from the giver's account into mine. Then and only then could I begin to draw on the $1,000,000. Only then would I be a millionaire. When the person handed me the check, I had two choices. I could put the check in a safe place and live my life working to earn $1,000,000; or I could cash the check and access the $1,000,000. I could use the resources given to me and I could be a millionaire.

When you were born into the kingdom of God, it is as if the Father handed you a check for your inheritance. You became a joint-heir with Jesus to the Father's riches. "Now if we are children, then we are heirs—heirs of God and co-heirs with Christ" (Rom. 8:17). Now you have two choices. You may begin to live on your inheritance, or you may live as if you are a servant rather than a child. You may live as if the inheritance did not belong to you.

As you boldly obey the present-tense voice of the Father, you access His power and provision. As you live the life to which you were born, you live in your inheritance. When faith is exercised on the earth, the power of God is released into the situation.

The eleventh chapter of Hebrews is about faith. Most of the chapter is about how faith looks in the lives of real people.

"By faith Abel offered God a better sacrifice than Cain did" (v. 4). How did Abel know what sacrifice would please God? He knew because God told him.[1] Abel acted on what God told him. His obedience was called faith.

"By faith Noah.. built an ark" (v.7). How did Noah decide to build an ark? Did he say to himself, "I think God would be pleased if I just dropped everything and built an ark. You never know when an ark might come in handy." No—God told Noah to build an ark. The story of Noah found in Genesis says over and over, "And Noah did all that the Lord commanded him" (Gen. 7:5). God calls this faith.

"By faith Abraham, when called to go... obeyed and went" (v. 8). Who initiated Abraham's journey? God called Abraham; Abraham obeyed; God called it faith.

In each case, God initiated the call and the faith-hero responded in obedience to God's present-tense voice. In every case, the obedience provided God the opportunity to show His power on earth.

## Faith Releases the Power of God

"By faith they passed through the Red Sea as on dry land" (v. 29). Moses led the children of Israel out of Egypt. Following God's voice, they found themselves in an impossible situation. As they were camped by the Red Sea, they looked up to see Pharoah's army advancing toward them. Looking at the situation in the material realm, they saw no escape. Moses, however, wasn't looking at the material realm. "He persevered because he saw him who is invisible" (v. 27). Moses had spiritual vision.

Read Exodus 14:1-12. You will see that God was leading the Israelites into this seemingly impossible situation for a definite purpose: "'I will gain glory for myself through Pharoah and all his army and the Egyptians will know that I am the Lord'" (Ex. 14:4). God already had a plan. He knew what He wanted to do to save Israel. He had already planned to open the Red Sea and let Israel cross over on dry land. However, He didn't just do it. He said to Moses, "'Raise your staff and stretch out your hand over the sea to divide the water so the Israelites can go through the sea on dry ground.'...Then Moses stretched out his hand over the sea, and all that night the Lord drove the sea back... and turned it into dry ground" (Ex. 14:15-22).

What drove the sea back and turned it into dry land? It was not Moses' staff. Moses' staff had no power. God drove the sea back. When Moses obeyed the present-tense voice of the Father, when he exercised faith, the power and provision of God showed up on the earth. Moses' faith-based obedience brought the fulfillment of the promise. The promise came by faith.

A similar incident occurred during Joshua's term of leadership. The story is found in Joshua 3. The Israelites needed to cross over the Jordan River. God said to Joshua: "'Tell the priests who carry the ark of the covenant: 'When you reach the edge of the Jordan's waters, go and stand in the river'" (Josh. 3:8). What happened when they obeyed the present-tense voice of God? "As soon as the priests who carried the ark reached the Jordan and their feet touched the water's edge, the water from upstream stopped flowing. It piled up in a heap a great distance away" (Josh. 3:15-16). Faith released the power and provision of God. The promise came by faith.

Luke tells us a story from the life of Christ in the seventeenth chapter of his gospel. Jesus was on His way to Jerusalem, and as He was going into a certain village, ten lepers met Him and called out to Him for mercy. "When he saw them, he said, 'Go, show yourselves to the priests'" (Luke 17:14). Put yourself in the lepers' shoes. They didn't know how this story would unfold. All they knew was that Jesus had told them to go show themselves to the priests. "And *as they went*, they were cleansed" (Luke 17:14b). Their obedience to the present-tense voice of Jesus released the power and provision of God. The promise came by faith.

God made a promise to Joshua. He said, "I will give you every place *where you set your foot*" (Josh. 1:3). As Joshua moved forward, God's power would meet him at every step. So it is with you and with me. As we move forward in response to God's voice, as we live by faith, the power of God will be released in our lives. The promise will come by faith.

## Faith: The Substance

"Faith is the substance of things hoped for" (Heb. 11:1, KJV). The writer of Hebrews uses language in this statement that might be used to state a scientific formula. The word translated "substance" means *that which stands under; the essence or make-up of.* We would use this word to say, for example, "$H_2O$ is the substance of water."

$H_2O$ *is the substance of* water.

$(H_2O) = (water)$

**Every time H+H+O come together—every single time without fail—water results.**

**Why? Because $H_2O$ *is the substance of* water.**

Follow the same logic as we look at the statement, "Faith is the substance of things hoped for." We can reduce the phrase "things hoped for" to "the promises of God" or "the vision." What can we hope for? What God has promised. How has He reinforced His promises? By implanting vision. (things hoped for) = (the vision)

Faith *is the substance of* the vision.

(Faith) = (the vision)

Every time faith is exercised on the earth—every single time without fail—the vision results. Why? Because *faith is the substance of things hoped for.*

The promises of God come from the spiritual end of the continuum of reality, heaven, to the material end of the continuum, earth, by the exercise of faith. Faith is the midwife of vision. Acting on the present-tense voice of the Father releases the power and provision of God on the earth.

The call that God has placed in your life, the vision that He has implanted in your imagination, is also a promise. He will bring it about. He will provide for every need in relation to the call. He will provide your passion, your insight, your clear understanding. He will open every door. He will give the finances. He will provide what you need when you need it as you walk out the call, always listening to His now-speaking voice. Every time you act in faith you give substance to God's promises. "And God is able to make all grace abound to you, so that in all things at all times having all that you need, you will abound in every good work" (2 Cor. 9:8).

## Faith: The Evidence

"Faith is... the evidence of things not seen" (Heb. 11:1, KJV). The writer of Hebrews uses a word translated "evidence," that means *convincing proof; to prove by demonstrating.* We might use the same word to say, "The experiment is the evidence of the thesis" or "The experiment proves the thesis."

The experiment provides convincing evidence that the thesis is true.

The experiment is *the evidence of* the thesis.

The experiment *proves* the thesis.

Every time the experiment is performed—every single time without fail— the thesis is substantiated.

Why? Because the experiment *is the evidence of* the thesis.

Follow the same logic as we look at the statement, "Faith is the evidence of things not seen." The phrase "things not seen" can be reduced to"the vision." The things for which we hope because God has promised them to us and has implanted in us the vision of them are the things not seen. (things not seen) = (the vision)

**Faith provides convincing evidence that the vision truly exists.**

**Faith** *is the evidence of* **the vision.**

**Faith** *proves* **the vision.**

**Every time faith is exercised on the earth—every single time without fail—it gives God the opportunity to prove His promises.**

**Why? Because** *faith is the evidence of things not seen.*

Since the promise comes by faith, until faith is expressed, the promise will be blocked. Conversely, every time faith is expressed, the promise will become experience. Do you long for the promises of God to be part of your daily experience? Prove them. Act on the present-tense voice of the Father. Live by His Word. Make the confession of Mary your confession: "I am the Lord's servant. May it be to me as you have said" (Luke 1:38). Give God every opportunity to prove the vision.

## Practice Power Praying

What is it that God has written on your imagination? What desires grow stronger as you walk with Him? What one step is God impressing upon you to take? Remember, you are only responsible for one step—the one in front of you. Think in terms of one step, not a whole journey. God will lead you step by step.

**Make this prayer your own:**
Today's date _____

*Father,*
*I embrace the Son's Life in me now. I believe that*
*You can speak Your desires into me. I trust You*
*to counsel me and watch over me. I sense You*
*calling me to one step. I am taking that step out*
*of a heart that longs to know You and follow*
*You. Father, hear my heart's cry.*
*In Jesus' name.*

## Faith is Not Sight

"So we fix our eyes not on what is seen, but on what is unseen.... We live by faith, not by sight" (2 Cor. 4:18; 5:7). Paul contrasts "faith" and "sight." They are opposites, he says. He is saying that physical sight, being able to observe something with our earth-eyes, is not the ground and basis of what we know to be true. We can know things that we cannot see.

He also contrasts physical vision and spiritual vision. Obviously we cannot "fix our eyes...on what is unseen" unless he means our spiritual eyes. So we conclude that our spiritual eyes can see spiritual substance just like our earth-eyes can see material substance.

Faith is spiritual sight, but not physical sight. Faith produces an understanding that surpasses what we can understand by observing material facts. "By faith we understand that the universe was formed at God's command, so that what is seen was not made out of what was visible" (Heb. 11:3). Without faith—the organ through which we receive spiritual resources—we cannot understand the full truth. We will see only a fragment of reality.

For example, suppose that I decided that I want to understand the truth about light. I would observe light carefully over a period of time and would eventually reach a conclusion based on my observations. I would conclude that light is what I can see. If I can see it, it's light. If I can't see it, it's not light.

This conclusion would be so limited that it would be untrue. It would fall so far short of the truth about light that it would be false. You see, light includes in it elements and power that I cannot observe. Light rays include gamma rays, but I can't observe them with my eyes. Light includes x-rays, ultraviolet rays, infrared rays, radio waves—but I can't see them. If the spectrum of light were represented in a diagram eight inches long, only one quarter of one inch would represent visible light. If I decided to define light based on what I could see, I would never know the power of light.

The spectrum of our reality includes elements and power that I cannot see with my earth-eyes. Reality is made up of what I can see and what I can't see. My reality includes the power of God, the plans and purposes of God, the present-tense voice of God and the promises of God. The spectrum of my reality includes the sovereignty of God, the lordship and authority of Jesus, the work of the Spirit, angels, Satan and the hierarchy of Satan's realm. The portion of reality that I can see—earth and the circumstances of earth—are only a miniscule portion of the whole continuum of

## Spectrum of Light

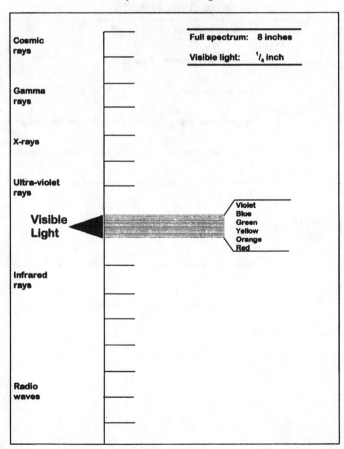

If I base my definition of reality on what I can observe on the earth, I will never comprehend the full reality. In the life of faith, circumstances never fully define reality.

Prayer impacts the invisible, spiritual end of the spectrum. The spiritual end of the spectrum impacts the material end. We are to focus our attention on what God is doing in the spiritual end of the spectrum of reality, confident that His activity will show up on the earth at the right time in the right way.

What we can observe from earth is only the appearance, it is not the truth. Faith acts in harmony with truth and disregards appearance.

### Spectrum of Reality

Sovereignty of God

Lordship and authority of Jesus

Power of the Spirit

Angels, surrounding the throne, crying "Holy, Holy, Holy"

Angels, ministering spirits sent to minister to the heirs of salvation

Angels fighting spiritual battles against the forces of Satan's realm

**Visible Reality** ◄ Earth: material, physical objects
Circumstances of earthly life

Satan: The spirit of rebellion now at work in the sons of disobedience

Powers, principalities, authorities of Satan's realm

| APPEARANCE | TRUTH | REALITY DEFINED |
|---|---|---|
| Loss | Gain | Philippians 3:7-8 |
| Troubles | Faith opportunities | James 1:2-4; Romans 5:3-5 |
| Impossible | Already in process | Romans 4:16-21 |
| Humiliation | Exaltation | Philippians 2:5-11; Hebrews 2:9 |
| Failure | Step forward | Psalm 119:71; Romans 8:28 |

How can one be expected to rejoice in tribulation? How can one be expected to consider all loss to be gain for the sake of Christ? How can one welcome trials as if they were friends? How can one confidently expect things that are impossible? The answer is to live in line with reality. Do not confuse appearance with truth. Don't be short-sighted. Don't be fooled by an optical illusion. Consider the following illustration.

In each illusion, what appears to be true is not true. In the first illusion, the parallel lines are straight, although they appear to be bent. In the second illusion, all three figures are the same size, although they appear to be different sizes. You cannot know the truth by appearances. You have to understand certain principles of visual perception. You have to understand how the background of each illusion impacts the way the foreground is perceived. Appearance is not truth.

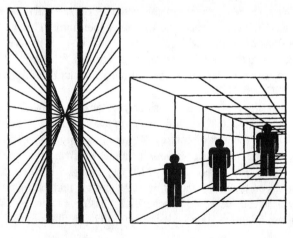

When you look at the circumstances of earth, what you see is no more reliable than the appearance of truth in an optical illusion. You have to understand the spiritual principles that stand behind the earth-circumstances in order to have the true perspective.

What are the circumstances in your life that look overwhelming and impossible? Now place them against the backdrop of the amazing power and astonishing love of God. Do they look different now? Do you see them as they are? Every circumstance, every need, every desire is God's entry point into your life. Every difficulty is simply highlighting the exact place where God will apply His power. Every challenge or obstacle is God's opportunity to substantiate His promises. Problems are nothing more than labor pains as God brings about the birth of His vision.

The truth is this: every mountain becomes a road. Every desert abounds with streams and pools of water. Lush gardens grow in the wastelands. Treasures are hidden in the darkness.[2]

## Faith is Not Work

"Anyone who enters God's rest, also rests from his own work, just as God did from his" (Heb. 4:10).

The life of faith is a life of rest. God intends for us to rest from our own work. In the life of faith, we rest in the fact that God is doing His work through us. We do not have to do the work. We are only the vehicle through which the work is done. We clothe His activity in the world.

Rest is not synonymous with inactivity. The person living a life of faith will be actively and aggressively living out the activity of Jesus. However, the person living the life of faith will live without anxiety, without insecurity, without uncertainty. This person's emotions and mind will be at rest. This person will live in the restful state that God has promised can be his. Jesus said, "'Come to me, all you who are weary and burdened, and I will give you rest'" (Matt. 11:28).

Consider your life. Consider your anxiety. What is causing you to be anxious? No doubt you are anxious about situations in which you feel out of control. You are probably anxious because you have circumstances in your life about which the outcome looks uncertain. You do not know which way things will turn out. How would you feel if you could be 100% certain that the outcome of any circumstance would be beneficial, pleasing, and perfect? Would that not alleviate your anxiety as the situation plays out? What if you knew for certain that no matter how things appear at any given moment, the outcome will be victory?

God calls things that are not as though they were. He talks about the eternal truth, not the appearance of the moment. God does not direct your attention to the need, but to the supply. Before a need enters your experience, God has fully prepared the supply. Your prayers (spoken faith) and your obedience (living faith) will get the finished work of God out of heaven and onto earth.

Consider the example of Joshua found in Joshua 6. In order to take possession of the land God had given them, the Israelites needed to take the city of Jericho. Jericho was protected by a high and impenetrable wall. "Now Jericho was tightly shut up because of the Israelites. No one went out and no one came in" (Josh. 6:1). What would collapse the walls of Jericho? Would military might? Physical strength? Clever strategy? Courage?

None of these things would do the job. It would take a mightier force than existed in the material realm. "By faith the walls of Jericho fell" (Heb. 11:30). Nothing but faith would collapse the fortress around Jericho.

How did this wall-tumbling faith operate? "Then the Lord said to Joshua, 'See, I have delivered Jericho into your hands'" (Josh. 6:2). In the material realm, nothing had changed. Jericho's wall was just as strong as it had always been. The odds were against Israel—or so it appeared. Notice that God did not say "I *will deliver* Jericho," but "I *have delivered* Jericho into your hands." God called what was not as though it were. Then He told Joshua exactly how to bring the victory out of heaven and establish it on the earth. You can read God's directives in verses 3-5. Joshua and the people did exactly as God had commanded. They were obedient to the present-tense voice of God. God called it faith, and it brought the promise. "By faith the walls of Jericho fell, after the people marched around them for seven days" (Heb. 11:30). Wall-tumbling faith is lived out in dynamic, active, bold obedience to God's voice.

Look at the coinciding of rest and activity. Activity directed by God will be carried out with our emotions and minds at rest in His promised outcome. When experiencing the rest of faith, anxiety need not be part of any situation. Face any experience with Christ's word: "'Take heart! I *have overcome* the world'"(John 16:33).

Perhaps you are feeling anxious, but are trying not to. Maybe you are working hard to have faith. You are anxious about your anxiety. Your very effort to stop worrying is blocking the flow of faith. Stop working at having faith. Rest from your own work. Self-effort cancels out faith.

Remember that the Life of Jesus is flowing through you. Allow Him to express His faith through you. Let Him show you everything that belongs to you. Your self-effort is cutting off the flow of His Life as surely as a tourniquet would cut off the flow of blood. Keep in mind that you are praying through Him and He is praying through you. Relax. Rest.

## How Does Faith Come?

The promise comes by faith, but how does faith come? "Faith comes from hearing" (Rom. 10:17).

Paul writes in Romans 10:17 that faith comes from hearing, using a word that means *the faculty of hearing.* In other words, faith comes by being able to hear. He is talking about spiritual hearing. Otherwise, all who have the ability to hear with appendages on the sides of their heads would have faith.[3] Jesus made it clear that not all could "hear" His message. "'He who has ears, let him hear'" (Matt. 11:15).

Romans 10:17 goes on to say, "Faith comes from hearing the message, and the message is heard through the word of Christ." The kind of hearing that produces faith comes *by means of* or *through* the "rhema" (word) of Christ. "Rhema," remember, means *the now-speaking word.* As the living Jesus speaks His message to spirit-ears, faith is produced. Jesus speaks faith. His voice stimulates your faith-organ to receive His provision.

## Faith is Born of First-hand Experience With God

When scripture tells us how to know God, it uses "sense" words.

Taste and see that the Lord is good (Ps. 34:8).

How sweet are your promises to my taste, sweeter than honey to my mouth! (Ps. 119:103).

I pray also that the eyes of your heart may be enlightened in order that you may know...(Eph. 1:18).

The Sovereign Lord has opened my ears (Is. 50:5).

> For we are to God the aroma of Christ (2 Cor.
> 2:15).

Why do you suppose God uses these sense words to tell us how to know Him? Consider this: how would you describe the taste of a fresh strawberry in such a way that someone who has never tasted a fresh strawberry would know how it tastes? You couldn't. A strawberry tastes like a strawberry. Things that we know through our senses, we have to learn first-hand. You could not describe the smell of the ocean to someone who has never smelled the ocean. You can't describe the sound of a thunderstorm to someone who has never heard a thunderstorm.

So it is with knowing God. You can only know Him by first-hand experience. Knowing God produces faith. You cannot trust the promises. You must trust the Promiser. A promise is only as reliable as the person who makes it. If you don't know the promiser, you have no way of knowing whether or not to rely on the promise. "Let us hold unswervingly to the hope we profess, for *he who promised* is faithful" Heb. 10:23). In order to live by faith, we have to be "fully persuaded that God [has] the power to do what He [has] promised" (Rom. 4:21).

Faith can only come through a direct, first-hand encounter with Jesus. Belief can come through second-hand information, but belief is not faith. I can believe things without putting my faith in them. For example, I can believe that a chair will hold me up. However, if I never sit in the chair—if I never put my faith in it—I will never move from belief to certain knowledge. "Faith is *being sure* of what we hope for and *certain* of what we do not see" (Heb. 11:1). Why does it matter whether I have belief or faith?

Let's say that I believe a certain chair will hold me up, but I have never sat in that chair. I am in the "belief" position. Now my adversary can say, "That chair will never hold you up."

"Of course it will. I believe it will," I reply.

"How do you know?" my adversary taunts.

"Because I can see that it is constructed of sturdy materials. I can see where the center of gravity would be. I'm sure the chair would hold me up."

Then my adversary could say, "But there may be a hidden flaw you don't know about."

My only answer could be, "You're right. There could be."

Belief can be shaken. Faith cannot.

Suppose that I take the faith position and sit in the chair. Now my adversary can say, "That chair will never hold you up." To which I will reply, "Of course it will."

My adversary will then say, "How do you know?" And I will reply, "Because it is." I will overcome his attack with the word of my testimony.[4] Faith cannot be shaken. Faith comes from first-hand experience.

Suppose that I came to earth from another planet with the assignment of learning all I can about the earth. Suppose that I wanted to learn about earth-rocks. Someone tells me, "Earth-rocks are hard." That becomes what I believe. With all my heart, I believe that earth-rocks are hard. However, no matter how much emotion I invest in my belief, it is only belief. It came to me second-hand and second-hand information can only produce belief.

Suppose that someone else told me later that earth-rocks are soft and spongy. Now what would I believe? I'd sometimes lean toward believing that rocks were hard, and other times I'd be convinced that they were soft. I'd be like a wave of the sea, blown and tossed by the wind.[5] I'd waver between two opinions.[6]

What would be the one and only remedy for my dilemma? I would have to touch an earth-rock for myself. Then I would know—not just believe—that earth-rocks are hard. Never again would I wonder if they're really soft. I would have faith that earth-rocks are hard. Faith cannot be shaken.

If you find yourself shifting back and forth between confidence and anxiety, if you find that your mind and emotions can never fully be at rest, probably you have strong belief, but have not moved on to faith. You cannot get faith from any source except God Himself. Get to know the Promiser for yourself, and it will be easy to trust His promises. Give Him every opportunity to prove Himself strong in your behalf. Let Him take responsibility for moving you on to faith. Rest in Him.

**Practice Power Praying**

"Faith that believes God will do what you ask is not born in a hurry; it is not born in the dust of the street, and the noise of the crowd. But I can tell where that faith will have a birthplace and keep growing stronger: in every heart that takes quiet time off habitually with God, and listens to his voice in his word. Into that heart will come a

simple strong faith that the thing it is led to ask
shall be accomplished."
(*Quiet Talks On Prayer,* S.D. Gordon)[7]

Are you listening to Him? Are you allowing
Him to create faith? Are you willing to invest the
time required to sit at His feet and learn from Him?
Are you so hungry for Him that you will make time
with Him priority above all else?

**Make this prayer your own:**

Today's date_____

*Father,*

*Let me hear You speak. Teach me to recognize Your
voice. Create spiritual hunger in me. Cause me to
crave Your presence. I open myself to You. Do Your
work.*

*In Jesus' name.*

[1]The scripture implies that Cain also knew, but did not act on what he knew.(Gen. 4:6-7)

[2]Isaiah 41:17-20; 45:3; 49:11

[3]Paul's whole point in this passage (Rom. 10:14-21) is that although Israel heard, she did not believe. Her "hearing" did not bring faith, because her spiritual ears were closed.

[4]Rev. 12:11

[5]James 1:6

[6]1 Kings 18:21

[7]S.D. Gordon, *Quiet Talks on Prayer* (Barbour and Company, Inc., Urichsville, OH, 1984), pp.116-117.

The books referenced in this chapter can be ordered by using the order form at the back of this book.

# 7

# How Does God's Power Flow?

Faith is how the power of God gets into the circumstances of earth. Power flows from purity. "'If you remain in me and my words remain in you, ask whatever you wish and it will be given you'" (John 15:7).

>   (1) "If you remain in me and my words remain in you...": **the process of purity**
>   (2) "...ask whatever you wish and it will be given you.": **the promise of power**

Notice that the process of purity precedes the promise of power. Don't seek power. Seek purity.

What does Jesus say is the key to the purity from which power flows? He says, first, "if you remain in me." He clarifies what He means by this phrase in verse 10 of the same chapter. "'If you obey my commands, you will remain in my love, just as I have obeyed my Father's commands and remain in his love.'" Jesus said, in other words, "As a spirit-man in an earth-body, I have been able to live in unbroken communication with my Father, Who is Spirit, by uncompromising obedience. I have never unplugged from my Power Source. His Life has always been free to flow through Me. You can have the same power by living in uncompromising obedience to Me at all times. Remain in Me."

Second, Jesus says that the flow of power is maintained "if my words remain in you." Jesus uses a word translated "remain" that means *to stay or to dwell*. It is a verb that indicates life and action. Jesus says that His Word should live in you, take up residence in you. His Word should be at home in you. Paul writes similarly, "Let the word of Christ dwell in you richly" (Col. 3:16). The word translated "dwell" means *to take up a fixed position, to reside in.* Again, scripture uses a word that indicates life and action. Christ's words should be at home in you in all their richness. When His Word is at home in you, what does it accomplish? It cleanses and purifies. "'You are already clean because of the word I have spoken to you'" (John 15:3).

In Hebrews 4:12-13 we read, "For the word of God is living and active. Sharper than any double-edged sword, it penetrates even to dividing soul and spirit, joints and marrow; it judges the thoughts and attitudes of the heart. Nothing in all creation is hidden from God's sight. Everything is uncovered and laid bare before the eyes of him to whom we must give an account." The writer of Hebrews describes the power of God's Living Word as a surgeon's implement laying bare the inner secrets before God. Like a surgeon's tool, it wounds in order to heal. It cuts away that which is sapping vitality. It removes spiritual disease in order to let Life flow.

When we put His Word into our lives, He breathes Life into it. He does His work by His Word. Let Him speak His Word into your spirit-ears. It will be His detergent. His Word will wash you clean.

Jesus says that the process of purity is remaining in Him and letting His Words remain in you. "'If you remain in me and my words remain in you, ask whatever you wish and it will be given you. *This is to my Father's glory, that you bear much fruit, showing yourselves to be my disciples*'" (John 15:7-8). Jesus says that when you get what you pray for, it glorifies the Father because answered prayer is fruit that proves the flow of His power through you, marking you as His disciple. The Father wants to give you what you desire because it glorifies Him. Answered prayer is the lush fruit of the Vine.

When we obey Him continually and feed always on His Word, He purifies our desires—refines away impurities and alloys—so that what I desire and what He desires are the same thing.

| | |
|---|---|
| Ask <u>whatever you wish</u>, and it will be given you.( John 15:7) | If we ask anything <u>according to his will</u>...we know that we have what we asked of him. (1 John 5:14-15) |

The choices of our free will become the echo of His almighty plan. "It is God who works in you to will...his good purpose" (Phil. 2:13).

**(Whatever you wish) = (Anything according to His will)**

## Launderer's Soap

"Who can endure the day of his coming? Who can stand when he appears? For he will be like a refiner's fire or a launderer's soap. He will sit as a refiner and purifier of silver" (Malachi 3:2-3).

When the Messiah enters your life, He will do so with power—refining and washing and purifying. He will make you like pure silver.

We have already seen that He uses his Word as His detergent. We have already seen that He uses the blood of Jesus flowing through us as His detergent. We will look at two other detergents that God shows us in His Word: circumstances and temptation.

## Circumstances: God's Detergent

"For our light and momentary troubles are achieving for us an eternal weight of glory that far outweighs them all" (2 Cor. 4:17).

No circumstance reaches you without God's permission. God does not cause difficult circumstances. Difficulties do not come to you *because* you belong to Him. In fact, the opposite is true. God shields you from circumstances that would destroy or defeat you. By the time a circumstance enters your experience, the victory is already available. He always leads us in triumphal procession in Christ Jesus. He has already overcome the world.

When God evaluates a situation headed your way and determines that the benefit will outweigh the pain, only then does He give permission for that situation to occur in your life. As I write these words, I know that this truth is difficult to reconcile with the wrenching, deep pain that some circumstances have produced. If you evaluate and try to understand these circumstances in light of the appearance from the earth-perspective, you will self-destruct. This is exactly why Paul follows his statement with this advice: "So we fix our eyes not on what is seen, but on what is unseen. For what is seen is temporary, but what is unseen is eternal" (2 Cor. 4:18). You cannot look at the ebauche as if it were the finished work.

Has anything ever appeared to be more of a failure than Jesus hanging on the cross? From the earth-view, Jesus' humiliation and crucifixion were brought about by the decisions and actions of evil people who were actively opposing the will of God. However, Jesus saw it differently.

Jesus described the onset of His arrest, trial, public ridicule, and crucifixion this way: "'The time has come for the son of man to be glorified'" (John 12:23). Jesus knew that the road to His exaltation led through the crucifixion. He knew that resurrection does not come without crucifixion. When He arose from the dead and was seated in the heavenlies at the Father's right hand, His glorification would be complete. But its beginnings would look like failure.

He dreaded the road, but His eyes were fixed on the outcome. "'Now my heart is troubled and what shall I say? 'Father, save me from this hour?' No, it was for this very reason I came to this hour. Father, glorify your name!'" (John 12:27-28). Why could he endure the pain that led to the glory? Because His eyes were fixed on what is unseen. "Who for the joy set before him endured the cross, scorning its shame, and sat down at the right hand of the throne of God" (Heb. 12:2). Does the scripture tell us that Jesus skipped merrily through the degradation and shame of the cross? Do we see Him stoically enduring the physical anguish? Far from it! We see Him sweating drops of blood, praying in agony, wrestling with His human fears.

Jesus focused past the difficulty to the glory that far outweighed it. He recognized that God's sovereignty was in effect even in the midst of His agonizing situation. He told Pilate, "'You would have no power over me if it were not given to you from above'" (John 19:11). Although it looked as if He were a victim of the desires and choices of God's enemies, Jesus never felt victimized. "'I lay down my life—only to take it up again. No one takes it from me, but I lay it down of my own accord'" (John 10:17-18).

Whatever has happened to you in your life, you do not have to allow it to cripple you. You do not have to hide behind it to avoid living productively. You do not have to allow it to grow and choke out the hope that God is holding out toward you. You can change your vantage point and see it from eternity's perspective. You can see that in God's hand, garbage is transformed into treasure. You can allow Him to create good out of raw material that looks like evil. Let your pain drive you to His heart.

God is intent on purifying His children so that His Life can freely flow through us onto the earth. He knows that His ways are encoded into our spiritual DNA and that purity is the process by which joy and contentment become our habit. He wants us to be pure because He loves us so passionately and longs for intimacy. Every circumstance has been filtered through His blood-stained love.

## Practice Power Praying

Have you surrendered everything to His purposes? Would you do so now? You can be honest with God. You can tell Him your true feelings of anger and confusion. He does not require you to have acceptable feelings before you approach Him. Let Him in to your darkest night, your deepest hurt, your blackest anger. Let Him in so that He can heal.

**Make this prayer your own:**
Today's date_____

*Father,*
*I trust Your love. I trust Your commitment to me.*
*I trust you with my feelings and I trust you with*
*my circumstances. Use everything in my life for*
*Your purposes.*
*In Jesus' name.*

## Temptation: God's Detergent

"God is faithful; he will not let you be tempted beyond what you can bear" (1 Cor. 10:13).

Look carefully at what the scripture says about temptation: God will not *let you* be tempted beyond what you can bear. Do you see that God is in charge of what temptation reaches you? If God is in charge of what temptation reaches you, can temptation have any purpose but good? "All the ways of the Lord are loving and faithful for those who keep the demands of his covenant" (Ps. 25:10).[1] "You are good, and what you do is good" (Ps. 119: 68).

Everything in your life serves God's purposes. "Your laws endure to this day, for *all things serve you*" (Ps. 119:91). Everything —including temptation— serves God's purposes. What is God's purpose? What eternal good is He accomplishing by allowing temptation?

First, let me backtrack and clarify something. God is not tempting you. He is not the source of temptation. "When tempted, no one should say, 'God is tempting me.' For God cannot be tempted by evil, nor does he tempt anyone" (James 1:13). He, however, decides what temptation will be allowed to reach you.

What is God's purpose in allowing temptation? What is His goal?

95

## God's Goal: Purity

"If we confess our sins, he is faithful and just and will forgive our sins and purify us from all unrighteousness" (1 John 1:9). God wants to do more than forgive our sins! God wants to: (1) forgive our sins, and (2) purify us from all unrighteousness. The Word of God, then, specifies two categories of impurity. He says that He will deal with *sins* by forgiving them and with *unrighteousness* by purifying it. He will deal with the fruit (sins) and He will deal with the root that produces the fruit. Sins are the behaviors we engage in. Unrighteousness is the attitude of rebellion that causes us to sin. When He deals with the root, the fruit ceases to exist.

"'Woe to you, teachers of the law and Pharisees, you hypocrites! You clean the outside of the cup and dish, but inside they are full of greed and self-indulgence. Blind Pharisee! First clean the inside of the cup and dish, *and then the outside also will be clean*'" (Matt. 23:25-16). Jesus said that when the inside is clean the outside will be clean. We spend our energy trying to get rid of sins, when Jesus wants to uproot sin's source. God allows temptation in order to isolate, identify, and uproot unrighteousness.

## Consider Jesus

Jesus had no unrighteousness because He never let unrighteousness take root. He never once sinned because He had no unrighteousness. But as a human, He had the human needs and instincts through which unrighteousness can enter. This is why He could be tempted, unlike the Father, Who cannot be tempted. How did God use temptation to accomplish His purpose for Jesus?

"In bringing many sons to glory, it was fitting that God...should make the author of their salvation *perfect through suffering*" (Heb. 2:10). God made Jesus perfect through suffering. "Perfect" means *the bringing of a thing to that completeness of condition designed for it*. The writer of Hebrews is not saying that Jesus used to be sinful, then became sinless. He is saying that the man Jesus, the earth-man, grew and matured into His role as author of salvation for all who believe. God accomplished this maturing process through suffering.

"Although he was a son, he *learned obedience from what he suffered*, and once *made perfect*, he became the source of eternal salvation to all who obey him" (Heb. 5:8). Again, Jesus learned obedience. He was never disobedient, but He continually progressed to deeper levels of obedience as deeper levels were required. He progressed to the point where He could be "obedient unto death, even death on a cross." God trained His Son step by step. He trained Him in deeper levels of obedience through what He suffered.

Two times, then, we read that Jesus was matured through suffering. What kind of suffering did God use to mature Jesus? What did Jesus suffer that brought Him to that completeness of condition designed for Him? This is not referring to the suffering of the cross. This suffering had to produce maturity before He could go to the cross. Through suffering, He *became* the source of eternal salvation

We find the description of His suffering in the same passage. "Because he himself *suffered when he was tempted*, he is able to help those who are tempted" (Heb. 2:18). He suffered when He was tempted. Look more closely at this whole passage in Hebrews.

> During the days of Jesus' life on earth, he offered up prayers and petitions with loud cries and tears to the one who could save him from death, and he was heard because of his reverent submission. Although he was a son, he learned obedience from what he suffered, and once made perfect, he became the source of eternal salvation for all who obey him (Heb. 5:7-9).

During Jesus' earth-life, He prayed with passion ("loud cries and tears") to the One who could save Him from death. Does this refer to death on the cross? No. This sentence is talking about a habit of Jesus', not a one-time occurrence. This entire passage is describing the process of Jesus' training. By calling the Father "the one who could save him from death," the writer is giving us a hint about the content of these impassioned outpourings of prayer. Jesus is calling out to be saved from death—and God heard and responded. Jesus asked to be saved from death and the Father saved Him from death. You can see that this passage is not referring to His hours in Gethsemane. God did not withold death at that time. What kind of death is He asking to be saved from? The wages of sin—death. Jesus was crying out to be rescued from sin that would bring His mission to failure. This intense suffering, struggling against sin, taught Him deep obedience and forged Him into the author of eternal salvation.

## Jesus' Sin-immune Life

Reflect back to the picture of blood=life. Jesus blood is Jesus' Life. With that as our visual, we can understand why Jesus had to live out His Spirit-life in an earth-body in order to become our salvation. WE ARE SAVED BY HIS LIFE. His Life did not become available to us—did not flow through us—until He had finished the work God gave Him to do. God assigned Him to purify and perfect flesh, making it subject to Spirit. In order to carry out that assignment, He had to live in flesh. Philippians 2:6-7 tells us that Jesus took on the nature of a man. He took on a nature that could be tempted. He temporarily emptied Himself of that aspect of His God-nature that cannot be tempted. He had to be tempted in order to overcome (wrestle to the ground, triumph over) sin. He can now live a Life in me and in you that has met and overcome the sin-disease.

The earth-picture of this spirit-truth is immunity. Our physical blood is the battleground between the immune system and invaders such as viruses or bacteria. When illness invades your body, your blood produces antibodies specifically designed to defeat that exact invader. Once your blood has built up enough antibodies against a specific disease, that disease will never have the opportunity to develop in your bloodstream again. When you are exposed to that disease, it will be met with an army of destroyers already in place. You are immune.

Immunity works by employing the body's ability to build up antibodies against a specific invader, rendering the invader powerless in future encounters. Should the disease ever show up again, immunity is already in place. The disease has no time to procreate and invade the body before it is destroyed by the antibodies.

The disease that invades our lives is called sin. God wanted to defeat sin in each individual life. He longs for individuals to live again in the kind of relationship to Him that sin originally cut off. We can only relate to God in spirit, and the spiritual nature of man was destroyed when the first sin separated him from his Spirit Life-source. God Himself is never exposed to sin. He cannot be tempted by sin.[2] The Life of God cannot develop an immunity to sin because the sin disease has no access to Him. That's why He came in the form of man. So that He could place Himself within the reach of sin, combat it head-on, develop a spiritual immune system that could be passed on to all who would be born again and accept His Life as their own. He has overcome the sin disease and longs to transfuse you with His sin-immune Life.

God used temptation as a training ground for His Son. Jesus had to face and overcome temptation so that He could be the Victor. His Life had to develop immunity to sin by exposure to the sin-germ so that He could pass along to those who obey Him eternal salvation (freedom from the evil one). The Life that flows through you and me— His saving Life—has already conquered sin.[3]

## The Anatomy of a Sin

Temptation is not sin. Temptation does not have to lead to sin. However, no sin comes into being without temptation. What is the process by which temptation becomes sin?

"Each one is tempted when, by his own evil desire, he is dragged away and enticed. Then, after desire has conceived, it gives birth to sin" (James 1:13-15). In this passage, James is talking about temptation that is successful, or results in sin. He describes the process for us.

**"By *his own evil desire...*"**
*The word "evil" really means strong or intense. This strong or intense desire, at its foundation, is built into you by the Creator. He has created you with a deep need for love and acceptance so that you will seek and find love and acceptance in Him. This need is the foundation of every desire. However, our God-created desires become misdirected when we seek to have them met outside of God. Anything outside of God only meets the surface of the need and provides only temporary relief and must be repeated over and over again. "As when a hungry man dreams that he is eating, but he awakens and his hunger remains; as when a thirsty man dreams that he is drinking, but he awakens faint with his thirst unquenched" (Is. 29:8). We spend our resources on bread which does not satisfy. We devour, but are still hungry; we eat, but are not satisfied.*

*When we turn our strong and intense desire outward to the world, a pattern of behavior becomes fixed. The very need or desire that should have turned us to God has turned us away from Him. Instead of being freed from our need by having it eternally met, we become enslaved to our need by having it forever unsatisfied. We have, then, a misdirected desire. James calls it "an evil desire." It has taken root in you. It is a root of unrighteousness and it grows a fruit called sin.*

**"By his own evil desire, he is *dragged away* and *enticed.*"**
*This misdirected desire, this root, has developed a magnetic attraction to something in the world. We'll call the object or situation in the world a "stimulus." A stimulus in the world acts as a magnet to entice you and drag you away. Away from what? Away from Christ. I am "in Christ," but this stimulus drags me away.*

*The stimulus has no power of its own. What tempts one person does not tempt another. The power is not in the object or the occurrence in the world. The stimulus is neutral. Unless it is enticing, it cannot tempt. Its only power is the attraction it holds for you. It is your own misdirected desire dragging you away.*

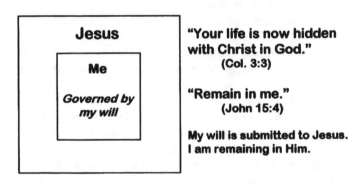

**"After desire *has conceived*, it *gives birth* to sin."**
*The root of unrighteousness in you mates with the stimulus in the world. The mating results in conception and sin is born. Sin is born of the mating between my misdirected desire and a stimulus in the world.*

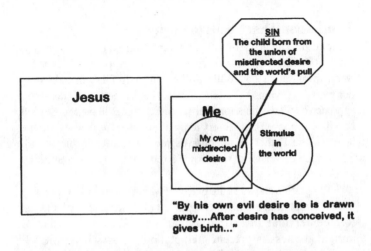

"By his own evil desire he is drawn away....After desire has conceived, it gives birth..."

*If one or the other did not exist, no mating could occur. It is unrealistic to think that the stimuli the world offers will disappear. Jesus said that we would have trouble in the world. He prayed that we not be removed from the world, but protected from its damaging influence. The stimuli in the world will not go away. Where does the answer lie?*

*The root of unrighteousness must be destroyed. Once the root is gone, the stimulus in the world has nothing with which to mate. The stimulus looses its power and becomes a neutral object. Once the inside is clean the outside will be clean also.*

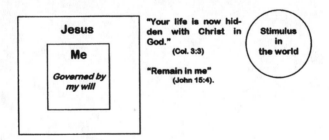

The root, the misdirected desire, is gone. The stimulus has nothing to mate with.

The stimulus loses its pull and becomes a neutral object. The stimulus has no power of its own, but is given power when it attaches to a misdirected desire.

The misdirected desire is the focus of God's purifying work.

101

## Temptation That Leads to Purity

Temptation can lead to sin, or temptation can lead to purity. Temptation forces choice. Every time we face temptation, we choose where to take our needs. Will we allow God to fulfill them and satisfy our eternal cravings? Or will we take the drive-through fast-food approach? Will we think long-term or quick fix? Will we choose God or will we choose Baal? Every temptation forces us deeper into the heart of the Father or anchors us more securely in the world. Temptation can cause us to become fixed in the way of the Spirit by persistent choice.

Temptation shows us the places at which we are still responsive to sin. Temptation is a heart ecogram. It pinpoints the weak places. Remember that the stimulus can only entice if a root of unrighteousness is present. Temptation exposes impurities. It unmasks our hearts so that sin cannot lurk there undetected. Temptation forces sin into the light where it can be destroyed.

"He was pierced for our transgressions, he was crushed for our iniquities" (Is. 53:5). Iniquities are the sins we commit. Transgressions are the inner roots of unrighteousnsess that produce sins, the attitude of rebellion. Scripture shows us repeatedly that Jesus not only dealt with sins, but also with the inner unrighteousness that produces sin.

| SCRIPTURE | SINS | UNRIGHTEOUSNESS |
|---|---|---|
| Romans 5:10 | reconciled through the death of his Son | saved through his life |
| Romans 6:5 | united with him in his death | also united with him in his resurrection |
| Romans 6:10 | death he died, he died to sin | life he lives, he lives to God |
| 1 John 1:9 | forgive us our sins | purify us from all unrighteousness |
| Isaiah 53:5 | crushed for our iniquities | pierced for our transgressions |
| Hebrews 5:1-6; 7:1-17 | Jesus: priest after the order of Aaron—to offer sacrifice on the altar to atone for sin | Jesus: priest after the order of Melchizedek—"on the basis of an indestructible life" |
| Hebrews 1:3 | provided purification for sins (died for sins on the cross) | sat down at the right hand of the majesty on high (lives and rules eternally) |

God allows temptation in order to get at the root of sin. Forgiveness of sins has been accomplished once for all at the cross. Purification from unrighteousness is an ongoing process— a process that is being accomplished by the Lord Himself.

**Practice Power Praying**

Does it seem that you continue to be confronted with temptations that expose a particular weakness? God is wanting to bring that weakness, that root, to the surface to clean it away. Would you actively cooperate with Him?

Next time the temptation comes, do not fight the stimulus. Do not turn your energies outward. Instead, let the Spirit identify the root. Turn that need or desire toward the Father. Ask Him to be your I Am.

**Make this prayer your own:**
Today's date_____
*Father,*
*I trust that You are watching over even the temptations that come to me. I know that Your purposes are only good. Teach me to how to make You the focus of all my desires and the supply for all my needs. Be my teacher.*
*In Jesus' name*

## Refined Like Silver

The Messiah will be like a refiner of silver. In the refining process, heat is applied. The silver and the impurities separate. The pure silver settles to the bottom and the impurities rise to the top where they can be skimmed off. This is what temptation does. It brings impurities to the surface so they can be removed. "The crucible for silver and the furnace for gold, but the Lord tests the heart" (Prov. 17:3). Do you see? What a crucible does for silver and what a furnace does for gold, God does for the heart.

God chooses the picture of silver to point us to His illustration in creation that teaches us about a pure heart. Silver is a perfect picture of what a pure heart will look like.

**Silver is the most malleable of all metals**. It can easily be hammered into new shapes. It is moldable.

A pure heart is soft, moldable and pliable in the hands of the Artist. "I will give you a new heart and put a new spirit in you; I will remove from you your heart of stone and give you a heart of flesh. And I will put my Spirit in you and move you to follow my decrees and be careful to keep my laws" (Ezek. 36:26-27). God will replace our hardened hearts with a soft spirit-heart—a heart that He can shape and mold to match His.

We are clay in the potter's hands. He can take our marred lives and make them into something else, "...shaping [us] as seems best to him" (Jer. 18:4). Listen to Him saying to you: "'Like clay in the hand of the potter, so are you in my hand'"(Jer. 18:6). He wants to mold you into someone beautiful and whole. He wants you to be His artwork. He wants your life to be an expression of His genius.

What hardens a heart? What makes a heart resistant to His work?

"Today, if you hear his voice, do not harden your heart" (Heb. 10:38). The word "hear" means *to hear and respond in the same action*. The Spirit emphasizes this when He says "Today." Every time we hear His voice and do not respond, our hearts become slightly hardened. The next time He speaks, it is harder to hear Him. Each time He speaks and we do not respond, the hardening progresses. Conversely, every time we hear His voice and do respond, our hearts become softer, more pliable. The next time He speaks, we hear Him more clearly. The softening progresses.

God, as always, takes the initiative. He speaks. "He wakens me morning by morning, wakens my ear to listen like one being taught. The Sovereign Lord has opened my ears, and I have not been rebellious; I have not drawn back" (Is. 50:4-5). The phrase, "to listen like one being taught" suggests to my imagination a student leaning forward to catch every word that falls from the teacher's lips. That's how God wants us to listen to Him— like one being taught. He wakens my ear, He opens (unstops) my ears. When I hear Him I do not draw back. I respond. Each time I respond, the callouses over my heart slough away until my heart becomes pure silver to be hammered into any shape He desires.

**Pure silver is the best conductor of heat and electricity of any element on earth**. A conductive substance is a substance through which power moves freely. By means of a conductor, power is transferred from one object to another.

A pure heart—a heart from which all alloys have been removed—is a conductor of God's power into lives and situations on earth. Jesus said, "'If anyone is thirsty, let him come to me and drink. Whoever believes in me, as the scripture has said, streams of water will flow from within him'" (John 7:37-38). Do you see? Drink from Him to quench your own thirst, then He will flow from within you in streams of living water. Your life will be the conductor of His Life.

Jesus uses another word that suggests conductive power. He says that He will "draw" people to Himself. He uses a word that suggests an almost irresistible force. God has given us a picture in His creation: magnetism. Think of Jesus in you as a magnet drawing the people in your world to Himself.

What happens when a conductive substance, let's imagine a paper clip, comes within the force field of a magnet? First, the paper clip is drawn to the magnet. Then, when the paper clip has attached to the magnet, the magnetic force begins to flow through it. The paper clip, the conductive substance, becomes a magnet. The magnet's power is flowing through the paper clip. If a second paper clip comes into contact with the first, it, too, will become a magnet because the magnetic force will flow from the first paper clip into the second.

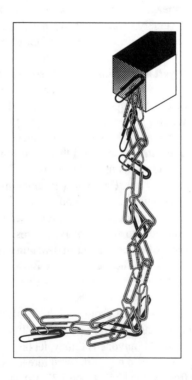

What happens if the first paper clip loses contact with the magnet? It loses its magnetism! It did not have power of its own; it only had the ability to conduct the magnet's power. It had induced magnetism. Apart from the magnet, the paper clip can do nothing.

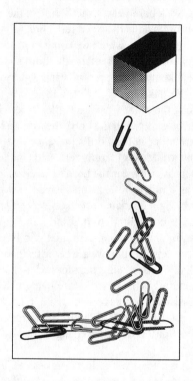

God does not give you power. He exercises His power through you. He has created you of a spirit-substance that is conductive. His power can flow through you.

Where is the epicenter of God's power on the earth? You know what the epicenter is. It's the place on the surface of the earth where the earthquake occurs. Everything else is the result of waves of power radiating out from the epicenter. Where is the epicenter of God's power on the earth? "Now unto him who is able to do immeasurably more than all we ask or imagine, according to *his power* that is at work *within us*" (Eph. 3:20). The epicenter of God's power is in you and in me. We are the conductors of the power of God.

God wants His power to flow through you in undiluted strength. He wants to rid you of anything that will hinder the flow. **Pure silver reflects light better than any other element.** Purified silver reflects without distortion.

The desires of a pure heart exactly reflect the desires of the Father. A pure heart is an undistorted reflection of His heart.

What is the process by which we come to reflect Him? "And we who with unveiled faces all reflect the Lord's glory, are being changed into his likeness with ever-increasing glory, which comes from the Lord, who is the Spirit" (2 Cor. 3:18).

Paul, in using the phrase "with unveiled face," is referring to Moses. When Moses met with the Lord, the skin on his face shone so brightly from being in the Lord's presence that Moses had to veil his countenance. Moses literally reflected God's glory. Paul is telling us that because we are in the Lord's presence, we, too, reflect His glory just as a mirror reflects an image. How does a mirror reflect? It absorbs light bouncing off an object and projects it back in exactly the same configuration. It absorbs and reflects.

As we absorb Him by being continually in His presence, we reflect Him. As we absorb Him, we are being changed into an exact reflection of Him. We are being transformed—changed from the inside out; structurally changed. We are being changed into His likeness progressively, "with ever-increasing glory." How is this changing being accomplished? "Which comes from the Lord, who is the Spirit." The Spirit is doing the changing as we continue in His presence.

A pure heart is a heart that reflects His desires. When my heart is pure, His desires are poured into my heart so that they become my desires and are expressed through my prayers. Impurity will distort the reflection, will cause it not to be exact. This is why the Father wants to make you pure. He wants you to desire your highest good. He wants to give you the desires of your heart.

**Silver is the metal most resistant to corrosion from the atmosphere.** Atmospheric corrosives cannot destroy silver, but can only produce surface tarnish.

A pure heart is resistant to corrosion and corruption by outside influences. "Do not conform any longer to the pattern of this world, but be transformed by the renewing of your mind. Then you will be able to test and approve what God's will is—his good, pleasing and perfect will" (Rom. 12:2).

Paul contrasts two ways of changing: conforming and being transformed. The word "conform" means *to be changed from outside or to be squeezed into a mold*. The word "transform" means *to be changed from within*. Both words mean to change forms, but one indicates change from the outside and one from the inside. Paul warns that the world wants to force you into a form that is not a natural fit. God wants to change your outward form so that it fits your inner being. He wants your inward self to be authentically reflected in your personality and lifestyle. His will for you is a perfect fit. The world's pattern is restrictive, diminishing, smothering. His will for you is beneficial and pleasing.

God wants to make you resistant to the forces and elements that would tarnish your beauty by trying to conform you to a pattern that does not fit you. He wants you to be forged into His image so that the corrosion in the world will not penetrate your life and diminish you. He will bring this about by renewing your mind—making your mind something different than it was before. Under His influence, you will begin to know, understand and embrace God's good, pleasing and perfect will.

Power flows from purity. Seek purity and you will find power.

[1]"Those who keep the demands of his covenant" are those who believe in the Lord Jesus Christ as their personal savior and who accept His perfect and eternal sacrifice as sufficient to assure their standing before God. This is the New Covenant demand: "to know you, the only true God, and Jesus Christ, whom you have sent" (John 17:3).

[2]James 1:13

[3]"As Adam never could have brought us under the power of sin and death, if he had not been our father, communicating to us his own nature, so Christ never could save us, except by taking our nature upon Him, doing in that nature all that we would need to do, had it been possible for us to deliver ourselves, and then communicating the fruit of what He effected as a nature within us to be the power of a new, an eternal life. As a divine necessity, without which there could be no salvation, as a n act of infinite love and condescension, the Son of God became a partaker of flesh and blood. So alone could He be the Second Adam, the Father of a new race."

Andrew Murray, *The Holiest of All* (Fleming H. Revell Company, Old Tappan, NJ), p. 96.

# ORDER FORM →

| TITLE | PRICE PER UNIT | TOTAL |
|-------|----------------|-------|
| *The Praying Life*<br>-J.K. Dean | $9.00 | |
| *Heart's Cry*<br>-J.K. Dean | $9.00 | |
| *Power Praying*<br>-J.K. Dean | $9.00 | |
| *Gleanings*<br>-J.K. Dean | $5.00 | |
| *Prayer*<br>-O. Hallesby | $5.00 | |
| *Let Us Pray*<br>-Watchman Nee | $5.00 | |
| *Quiet Talks ...*<br>-S.D.Gordon | $10.00 | |
| *The Saving Life...*<br>-Ian Thomas | $9.00 | |

| | | |
|---|---|---|
| | Sub-total | |
| **Shipping & handling**<br>Add $2.25 for first item and<br>.25 for each additional item. | Shipping<br>& handling | |
| Enclose a check for your order<br>or use your MC or VISA. | TOTAL<br>amount due | |

Make checks payable to:
*The Praying Life*
*Foundation.*

____MC ____VISA

Card #:

Expiration:

Sign:

_____

**Shipping address:**
**(PRINT LEGIBLY)**

**Name**_____

**Address**_____

_____

**Phone**_____

See next page.

111

☐ Add me to your newsletter mailing list.

☐ Send me information about how I can schedule Jennifer Kennedy Dean for a prayer conference or as a keynote speaker.

☐ I want to participate in seeing that the message of *Power Praying* reaches as many people as possible. I am enclosing my tax-deductible gift for your ministry in the amount of $_____.

Comments:

To order *Power Praying*, *The Praying Life*, or *Heart's Cry* in quantities for Bible studies, discipleship groups, or prayer groups, call:

## 1-800-917-BOOK

**The other titles on this order blank cannot be ordered through the 800#.**

---

Return this order blank to:

**The Praying Life Foundation
P.O. Box 62
Blue Springs, MO 64013**

---